An

Examination of

DISPENSATIONALISM

by

WILLIAM E. COX

AN EXAMINATION OF DISPENSATIONALISM

BY

WILLIAM E. COX

PRESBYTERIAN AND REFORMED PUBLISHING CO.
Phillipsburg, New Jersey

Library of Congress Catalogue Card Number LC 62-21165
ISBN: 0-87552-153-3
Printed in the United States of America

CONTENTS

INTRODUCTION

This book is sent forth, prayerfully, in the scriptural attitude of "Come, let us reason together." It is written by one who for a number of years was a dispensationalist. My entire background, from the time of my conversion at age sixteen until long after my call to the ministry, was one in which the Notes of the *Scofield Reference Bible* were looked on as being the final authority in any theological discussion. It was only after much doubt and searching of the Scriptures that I was constrained to leave such a fascinating school of interpretation.

Nor is this book written in order to attack any person or group. Rather, it is written to enlighten, and to encourage a mature study of the Bible on a subject which demands the attention of every interested Christian. I have many close friends who remain in the dispensational school, friends whom I respect and love in the Lord. These friends know me as a very conservative evangelical preacher. They also know that my pulpit ministry has always had a prophetic note about it, and that I often preach the literal, visible, bodily second coming of our Lord as the Blessed Hope of all believers. I believe very definitely in predictive prophecy, and accept the entire Bible, without apology, as the infallible Word of God.

In my book, *The New-Covenant Israel*, futurism and dispensationalism were treated as though they were synonymous terms. The scope of that book would not have permitted a more detailed distinction. While futurism is restricted for the most part to national Israel, dispensationalism covers a much broader field. Therefore, it seems important that a separate book be devoted to dispensationalism.

Dispensationalism holds many beliefs in common with both futurism and premillennialism. Each of the three schools, however, hold some beliefs distinctive to itself. To discuss every teaching held by the different groups of dispensationalists would require a book within itself, because of the many ramifications of dispensational teachings. For example, Jesse Wilson Hodges (*Christ's Kingdom and Coming*, pp. 34-39) lists twenty-seven distinct dispensational teachings, and by no means covers the field. It shall be our purpose to deal with the more cardinal doctrines of dispensationalism. Many of their minor points will be covered under the larger headings.

Dispensationalism, although a comparatively new doctrine, is put forth arrogantly as the only true approach to Bible study and interpretation. And, while this belief is that of only a small minority of Christians, those who do not go along with it are often castigated as liberals. Although no major denomination, to my knowledge, sanctions either dispensationalism or the *Scofield Reference Bible*, serious divisions have been caused in just about every major denomination by both. *An Examination of Dispensationalism* is sent forth, not as an attack against dispensationalists, but rather as a defense of the beliefs and integrity of the great majority of Christians on this particular subject. The beliefs defended in this book are sincerely looked upon by this writer as being the faith once delivered to the saints and recorded in the New Testament. Our paramount concern throughout the book is: "What *saith* the scripture?" (Romans 4:3).

The book is written for laymen and ministers alike. Technical theological language has been kept to a minimum. Scholarliness is claimed neither for the writer nor for the book. It is hoped that the work will serve a useful purpose in view of the increased theological interest among laymen. Unless otherwise indicated, all Scripture passages are from the American Standard Version of the Bible published in 1901 by Thomas Nelson & Sons.

I
DISPENSATIONALISM

Dispensationalism, as we know it today, had its beginning with the Brethren movement, which became prominent around 1830. This group came to be known as "Plymouth Brethren," because their publications centered in Plymouth, England. Ever since the days of John Nelson Darby, dispensationalists have been prolific writers, and their works are in abundance today.

The Brethren movement constituted a radical change from the historic teachings of Christianity. This group claimed to have "rediscovered truths" which had been lost sight of since the days of the apostles. Although the Plymouth Brethren are a very small sect, their "rediscovered truths" are to be found in nearly every Christian denomination. This is mostly because of the great influence of the *Scofield Reference Bible*, which was written to perpetuate these views after Scofield had come under the influence of Darby. Over two million copies of this "Bible" have been sold since its publication in 1909.

According to Oswald T. Allis (*Prophecy and the Church*), W. E. Blackstone's book, *Jesus is Coming*, also did much to spread the Brethren views among Christians in America. Several hundred thousand copies of this book were mailed out gratis to Christian workers during the early part of this century.

The Brethren boasted, from their very beginning in the nineteenth century, that their teachings represented a wide departure from the doctrines of their predecessors and contemporaries. According to them, all the prominent commentaries, all the church fathers, and even the Reformers, were deluded by "man-made doctrines," while only the Brethren were subject to and submissive to the Bible as the Word of God. That this superior attitude has not changed in our day is evident from the following quotations from dispensationalists.

In a recent book (*When the King Comes Back*, pp. 13, 14) Oswald J. Smith, in one sweeping statement, attempts to discredit all major commentaries because these commentaries are not in agreement with his views:

> I know very few of the old commentaries that are trustworthy when it comes to prophecy. Nearly all of them spiritualize the predictions of the Old Testament prophets and confuse the kingdom with the Church. Hence *their interpretations are worthless* (italics mine).

1

Having quoted Isaiah 11:1-13; 12:1-6 (on page 63 of the same book), Smith says of these passages:

> None of it was fulfilled at the first advent, and none of it can be spiritualized, for it has no fulfillment in the Church, *in spite of what the great commentators say. God did not see fit to enlighten them* (italics mine).

The *Scofield Bible* also cautions its readers that its teachings are the opposite of those of historic Christianity, those historic teachings being untrustworthy. The reader is told that as he studies the Gospels he must free his mind from the beliefs *that the church is the true Israel*, and that the Old Testament foreview of the kingdom is fulfilled in the church. Scofield admitted that this belief was "a legacy in Protestant thought" (p. 989).

In speaking of the dispensational teaching that the church was not prophesied in the Old Testament, Harry A. Ironside (*Mysteries of God*, p. 50) boasts of the fact that this teaching was non-existent until introduced by John Darby in the nineteenth century.

> In fact, until brought to the fore, through the writings and preaching of a distinguished ex-clergyman, Mr. J. N. Darby, in the early part of the last century, it is scarcely to be found in a single book or sermon throughout a period of 1600 years! If any doubt this statement, let them search, as the writer has in a measure done, the remarks of the so-called Fathers, both pre and post-Nicene, the theological treatises of the scholastic divines, Roman Catholic writers of all shades of thought; the literature of the Reformation; the sermons and expositions of the Puritans; and the general theological works of the day. He will find the "mystery" conspicuous by its absence.

Writing in the introduction of a book by Lewis Sperry Chafer (*The Kingdom in History and Prophecy*, p. 5), Scofield said:

> Protestant theology has very generally taught that all the kingdom promises, and even the great Davidic covenant itself, are to be fulfilled in and through the Church. The confusion thus created has been still further darkened by the failure to distinguish the different phases of the kingdom truth indicated by the expression "kingdom of Heaven," and "kingdom of God."

John Walvoord, in an article in *Bibliotheca Sacra* (Jan.-Mar., 1951, p. 11) points up the fact that his millennial thinking is a departure from that of the great Reformation theologians.

> Reformed-eschatology has been predominantly Amillennial. Most if not all the leaders of the Protestant Reformation were Amillennial in their eschatology, following the teachings of Augustine.

2

These quotations serve to prove at least two things concerning dispensational theologians: (1) their actual contempt for the thinking of historic Christian theologians, and (2) the fact that dispensational doctrines (note especially their teaching that the church is separate from Israel) are of comparatively recent origin.

Present-day dispensationalists are of necessity premillennialists. The doctrine of premillennialism, however, is much older than the doctrine of dispensationalism. Historic premillennialism can be traced back to the early post-apostolic history of the church, while, as stated before, modern dispensationalism originated in the early nineteenth century. Historic premillennialism had no teaching whatsoever of a future hope for Israel outside the church; such a separate future hope for Israel is the main teaching in modern dispensationalism. Oswald T. Allis (*Prophecy and the Church*, pp. 8, 9) lists nine features of dispensationalism and goes on to state correctly that not more than two of these were held by historic premillennialism.

Historic premillennialism could be defined simply as the belief, based on an interpretation of Revelation 20:1-10, that there will be an earthly reign of Christ following his second coming. This was believed to be a perfect peaceful reign, during which time perfect laws, justice, and tranquillity were to prevail because Satan would be bound and therefore unable to lead people into sinful pursuits. This school of thought held that there would be two resurrections, which were to be separated by a period of one thousand years. At the first resurrection all saints would be rewarded; at the second all the unsaved would be judged and punished. Every believer of every age was to be resurrected at the first resurrection, and every believer (having been made a part of the church) would take part in the earthly reign of Christ.

So it is unfair and untrue for modern dispensationalists to claim to be the champions of premillennialism. While all dispensationalists are of necessity premillennialists and futurists, it does not follow that all premillennialists, nor even all futurists, are dispensationalists. Both dispensationalism and futurism are merely recent additions (and foreign elements at that) to historic premillennialism. Both new theories seem to have originated during the nineteenth century.

Before examining the beliefs of the dispensationalists, which differ so radically from the historic Christian teachings, let us

3

satisfy our curiosity as to how these radical changes in doctrine could gain such wide influence, even breaking across denominational lines and flying in the face of accepted creeds. I believe the answer to this dilemma can be gained by taking the spiritual pulse of Darby's generation.

A study of the early nineteenth century reveals that doctrinal preaching was all but unheard of, and any emphasis on the second coming of our Lord was held up to ridicule by the clergy. Liberalism was in vogue, and lethargy had crept into the churches. The pulpits were filled by "professional" clergymen, and the people were "like sheep without a shepherd." Lay-people were being spiritually starved. They longed for some sure word of prophecy, but heard only horns with uncertain sounds from the pulpit Sunday after Sunday. In a climate such as this a natural by-product would be almost total ignorance with reference to things taught in the Bible. It was into such an incubator as this that Brethrenism was born.

It is not surprising that into such a spiritual vacuum there should arise, not only Darbyism, but all sorts of innovations. The Mormons were teaching chiliasm (millennialism) about the time of John Darby. Joseph Smith put out a book (*Book of Mormon*) in 1830—the same year which is recognized as marking the recognition of Darby as a leader among the Brethren. Smith, like Darby, taught a regathering of Israel. In 1831 William Miller (the founder of Adventism) began proclaiming his "findings." Miller set 1843 as the time the world would come to an end. Many of his followers sold their possessions and put on their robes to await the Lord's return. Judge Rutherford wrote a book entitled *Comfort for the Jews*. Rutherford was the successor to Charles Taze Russell, who founded Millennial Dawnism around 1880. Russell published his works beginning in 1881, the year before Darby's death. Rutherford's group has been known as "International Bible Students," "Russellites," and are best known to us today as "Jehovah's Witnesses." Their fantastic millennial theories are well-known and need no elaboration here.

This spiritual climate not only accounts for the ready acceptance of Darbyism, but it also lends insight into the direction taken by these "rediscovered truths." The Brethren teachings, with their emphasis on prophecy and the second coming of Christ, met a need in the lives of the spiritually-starved people of that generation. It is not difficult to replace a vacuum! If we should not be surprised that Darbyism met with a ready response in such surroundings, neither should we be surprised if the people of that generation—with their lack of biblical teachings—passed all of Darby's spiritual "legislation" even though many of the bills in his legislation contained "riders" (strange innovations). Darby not only returned to the faith once delivered to the saints—which admittedly had been discarded and needed to be recovered—but he went far beyond that faith, bringing in many teachings of his own, which were never heard of until he brought them forth. The words of Lewis Sperry Chafer, himself an outstanding dispensationalist, would seem to be very appropriate at this point (*The Kingdom in History and Prophecy*, p. 14): "Satan's lies are always garnished with truth and how much more attractive they seem to be when that garnishing is a neglected truth!"

II

JOHN DARBY

It is impossible to understand fully the dispensational view of eschatology apart from some history of its origin and main spokesmen. Biographers of John Darby refer to him as the father of modern dispensationalism.

Around 1825 many dissenting groups were beginning to pull away from the established churches in different parts of Europe. The three paramount centers seem to have been Dublin, Ireland, and Plymouth and Bristol in England. The leaders of this movement recognized the pen as being "mightier than the sword," and turned out an abundance of literature publicizing their new beliefs. Darby referred to the church as "the Brethren." The headquarters for the printing of the Brethren was in Plymouth. Thus, it followed naturally for this new denomination to be called Plymouth Brethren, and the name stuck.

Darby was not the founder of the Brethren movement, although he became its dominant leader and shaped its history. Even though there were many great names associated with the movement, they all were dwarfed, and his name continues in the minds of friend and foe alike. By 1830 he was in complete control of the movement and definitely shaped its dispensational doctrines. That his leadership was unshakable is evident from the fact that, although he made many bitter enemies among the founders of the movement, no man was able to unseat him. Many indeed tried, but themselves were forced either to buckle to Darby or leave the group.

The "father of modern dispensationalism" was born John Nelson Darby in Ireland, in the year 1800, and died in 1882. He was an honor student in Westminster and Trinity college, where he studied law. He was a successful lawyer until the age of twenty-seven, at which time he gave up his law practice to become a curate in the Church of England. He followed this profession until the time he joined the Brethren movement about 1827.

Darby's biographers say he was eccentric, homely, crippled, and had a deformed face, yet that he possessed a magnetic personality and a keen organizing ability. The man was indefatigable,

6

having been known to travel, it is said, for days while living on acorns. He came from a family background of education, culture, and social standing. He apparently was blessed with a keen mind. William Blair Neatby, who was critical of the movement headed by Darby, described him (*A History of the Plymouth Brethren*, p. 192) as follows:

> No doubt Darby had many perfectly intelligible titles to success. His attainments were great and varied, apart from his classical and theological scholarship. He could write and speak in several modern languages, and translated the whole Bible into French and German.

While convalescing from injuries received when his horse threw him, Darby was convinced of the authority of Scripture and the importance of prophetic teachings. He was especially impressed by the thirty-second chapter of Isaiah, which he referred to as describing "a state of things in no way established as yet."

In spite of his belief in the authority of the Scriptures, Darby retained some of his old Anglican beliefs. For example, Neatby says of him (*ibid.*, p. 63): ". . . Darby alone among the earlier Brethren remained a pedobaptist."

Darby wrote into the doctrinal platform of the Brethren one innovation which still marks the dispensational school today. We refer to his disregard of and actual contempt for history. In his book, *Prophecy and the Church*, p. 26, Allis quotes Darby as having said:

> I do not want history to tell me Nineveh or Babylon is ruined or Jerusalem in the hands of the Gentiles. I do not admit history to be, in any sense, necessary to the understanding of prophecy.

The Plymouth Brethren, when first organized, had two main distinctives: (1) theirs was an ecumenical movement, and (2) they sought to do away with an ordained clergy and anything which even resembled organization within the local church. They were opposed to music or any type of ritual in the church service. Darby's watchword, according to his biographers, was "the union of the children of God." The Brethren frowned on ordination as constituting a man-made ministry, and the very word "Brethren" was an attempt to get away from denominationalism.

While the subject of the Lord's second coming soon came to dominate the dispensational school, it scarcely entered into their thinking at the very first. Their two main starting aims—ecumenicity, and looseness of organization—may be seen from the following quotations.

> We should come together in all simplicity as disciples, not waiting on any pulpit or ministry, but trusting that the Lord would edify us together, by ministering as He pleased, and saw good from the midst of ourselves (Thomas S. Veitch, *The Brethren Movement*, p. 19).

> That ordination of any kind to preach the Gospel is no requirement of Scripture (Neatby, *op. cit.*, p. 26).

> Without any rules, desiring to act only as the Lord should be pleased to give light through His Word.

Following his break with the Church of England and his joining the Brethren movement, Darby, along with the rest of the Brethren, claimed to have been given many "rediscovered truths." These alleged truths supposedly had been taught by the apostles, then lost sight of. Even the great Reformers had not known of these doctrines. These "rediscovered truths" were, in fact, the direct opposite of all historic Christian teachings proclaimed by the Reformers and extant commentaries. Notice was given to the world at large that everyone should look on all previous post-apostolic teachings as false, and that only the "rediscovered truths" of the Brethren should be embraced.

The main teachings of dispensationalism, which will be dealt with in subsequent chapters, contrasted with the historic Christian beliefs. Perhaps a summary of their beliefs would be in order at this point. The following quotation (Arnold Black Rhodes, editor, *The Church Faces the Isms*, p. 95) is pertinent.

> In brief, the teachings of dispensationalism are as follows:
> 1. The Jews are to be saved by repentance; they are to be left here on earth as God's earthly people
> 2. The Gentiles are to be saved by faith; they will be taken to heaven after the Rapture.
> 3. The church is a parenthesis in God's plan and will end in apostasy.
> 4. The kingdom of heaven and the kingdom of God are sharply differentiated, the first being the Davidic kingdom and the latter being God's universal world-wide kingdom.
> 5. God deals with men according to seven dispensations.

Only one of these five major doctrines of dispensationalism (number 2 above) in any way agrees with historic Christian teachings. Even that one would have to be explained, since historic Christians teach that, after the Rapture, Christians are to be taken to heaven *permanently*, whereas dispensationalists say it is only temporary at that time. Dispensationalists go on to teach that, after seven years, the church will be returned to earth, where it will take part in an earthly millennium. During the millennium, according to dispensationalists, the church will have a position inferior to that of Israel. They teach that, after the millennium, the church will be returned to heaven the second time, there to spend eternity while Israel remains forever on the earth. None of this, of course, is in agreement with historic Christian beliefs. And, whereas the dispensationalists include only the Gentile Christians in the Rapture, historic Christians would include *all believers* from every age and nationality.

The Brethren divided into two distinct groups after Darby came into their midst. These groups came to be known as "exclusive assemblies" and "open assemblies." Darby was the originator of the exclusive assemblies. In 1845 he returned to Plymouth from an extended stay in Switzerland. He and a Mr. Newton, who had been the pastor at Plymouth during Darby's long absence, had doctrinal differences. This resulted in a war—in both verbal and pamphlet forms. Newton's strong following in that particular church prevailed, and Darby "quit the assembly" with fifty or sixty members. This, according to Veitch, was the beginning of "exclusivism." Neatby said, concerning Darby's visit to Plymouth: "From the moment he decided to come, Brethrenism was doomed."

When Darby withdrew from the Plymouth assembly, he formed another assembly in the same town. This marked the beginning of the so-called exclusive assemblies. Exclusives claimed that their meeting in any place was the sole "expression of the church of God" there. It was divinely recognized, nothing else was! Darby wrote to a Mr. Spurr of Sheffield in 1854 regarding the case of a Mr. Goodall: "He is rejected in London . . . I take part in this act, and hold him to be outside the church of God on earth . . ."

The exclusives formed a federation of assemblies with a Central Meeting. This was, of course, contrary to the very founding principles of Brethrenism. Darby excused this by saying they had discovered that the New Testament favored an area church. This meant that although an area such as London might have many churches, they all composed one municipal Church. The Central Meeting was set up in London. This Central Meeting decided, for all the churches, all such questions as receiving members, cutting off assemblies, and so forth. Veitch says:

> These decisions were binding upon the area, and from the prestige
> which the London Meeting held, far beyond it. In the strong hands
> of Mr. Darby, the Central Meeting proved an instrument by which he
> controlled and dominated the assemblies (*op. cit.*, pp. 60, 61).

Only Darby's strong personality held the exclusive assemblies together. Neatby says: "When Darby's fiat ceased to be law the party was broken. When Darby died it was scattered like dust."

Darby, throughout his career as a religious leader, was an extremely controversial individualist. Once while debating with Dwight L. Moody, Darby angrily closed his Bible and refused to continue the public debate. He castigated Newton, even though Newton issued a pamphlet apologizing for doctrinal error. When Darby, on the other hand, was told that many of *his* teachings were looked on as heresy and were causing grief to many, he threatened to leave the fellowship rather than retract the teachings.

He excommunicated George Muller because Muller received members whom Darby did not approve. This in spite of the fact that these members had first been questioned by many pastors and other members. This is known as the "Bethesda Incident" to Darby's biographers. Darby wrote a circular from Leeds on August 26, 1848, cutting off from fellowship, not only all Bethesda members, but all assemblies who received any who had ever been members at Bethesda! Neatby called this circular: "A decree that was to spread strife, misery, and shame like a conflagration to the remotest bounds of Christiandom."

Darby finally approached Muller to heal the breach over the Bethesda incident. Muller said at that time: "I have this moment only ten minutes time, having an important engagement before me, and as you have acted so wickedly in this matter I cannot now enter into it as I have no time." These two former friends never saw each other again, and Darby continued to castigate Muller until his death.

Even some of Darby's best friends hesitated at some of his doctrines. He was accused of heresy a number of times. One particular case was his teaching that Jesus was sometimes caused to suffer at the hand of God simply for the sake of being punished. These teachings were recorded by Darby in 1858, when he wrote on "The Suffering of Christ," in which he stated the Lord suffered in a three-fold way. The third point was that Jesus endured sufferings at the hand of God which were *non-atoning!* When confronted with this teaching, Darby said it was not found in the New Testament, but in the Psalms. Darbyites today still claim to find things *implied* in the Old Testament which are not so much as mentioned in the New Testament.

Three things might be said in summary concerning this man with whom we differ so much:

1. He was able to do what he did only because there was a great need. One historian said of Darby: "His strength lay, now as ever, in the reality of the abuses he attacked." The church was corrupt, the clergy unconcerned. Liberalism had all but taken over. Prophetic teachings and sermons about the second coming of Christ were almost unheard of. Multitudes of people were spiritually starved and longed for biblical preaching and a message of hope. Darby was a man of the hour, and so the people heard him gladly.

2. John Darby, and the Plymouth Brethren in general, did much good for the church of Jesus Christ. They stimulated a much-needed interest in Bible study. They exposed abuses in the church of their day. And, as time went on, they emphasized the second coming of our Lord.

3. The same thing could well be said about the Brethren and Darby that Paul said about the Judaizers of his day. They had a zeal for God, "but not according to knowledge" (Romans 10:2). Many present-day evangelicals would agree with many of Darby's emphases, and certainly all of us would welcome his zeal for the cause of Christ. His zealousness, however, was not always based on a knowledge of the Scriptures, and, like the Sadducees of Jesus' day, he "erred, not *knowing* the Scriptures." Yet Darby's zeal plus his systematic legally-trained mind enabled him to carry the common people along with *all he proposed.* This was mostly because of the conditions, that is, the lack of Bible training among the laymen, their hunger for change, the lethargic "professionalism" among the established clergy of that day, and the like.

In looking at John Nelson Darby, the "father of modern dispensationalism," we have tried to paint the whole man—bringing out his many good points as well as what we sincerely consider to have been his unscriptural teachings. The following caution (W. G. Turner, *John Nelson Darby*, p. 62) would seem to be an appropriate conclusion for this chapter. Darby, according to Turner:

. . . commands the reverence and admiration of those who recognized in him a spiritual guide. But there is always need for caution lest this admiration of a Christian leader's intellect and spiritual qualities should be allowed to pass (unconsciously at first perhaps) into an unwarranted and dangerous deference to his authority, or even into peaceful acquiescence in all his teachings as though it were impossible for such a man to err in any point of faith or practice.

III

C. I. SCOFIELD

The father of dispensationalism, Darby, as well as his teachings, probably would be unheard of today were it not for his devoted follower, Scofield. The writer became increasingly aware of this fact as he did research for this book. Darby's books are gathering dust on the shelves of the comparatively few libraries stocking them. Information concerning him is scarce indeed.

Darby was a prolific writer, and also spent much time lecturing in different countries. Scofield came to know him and became enamored by his teachings. These two men had at least two things in common—both had practiced law, and both had untiring energy in advancing their beliefs. Scofield wrote many books, founded what is now called the Philadelphia College of the Bible, and, in 1909, published his *Scofield Reference Bible*. All these efforts inculcated the Plymouth Brethren teachings learned from Darby.

Cyrus Ingerson Scofield lived from August 19, 1843, until July 24, 1921. He was born in Michigan, but his family soon moved to Tennessee. While serving as a private in the Confederate Army, during the Civil War, he was decorated. Upon being discharged from the Army he took up law. He also entered politics and was appointed U. S. Attorney to Kansas by President Grant. During this period of his life he became a heavy drinker.

Scofield was converted in 1879, and three years later was ordained a Congregational minister. With no formal theological training he wrote his reference Bible. Except for this work, it is doubtful whether this man's name would be remembered any more than would Darby's. Taking the King James Bible and adding his own Notes to it, he assured himself a place in the memory of all who read that version of the Bible. This was in violation of the policy of all well-known Bible societies, whose rules have been: "Without Note or Comment." Certainly Scofield was ignoring John the Revelator's warning about adding or taking from his prophecy (Rev. 22:19), for he did not hesitate to pry apart John's verses and intersperse his own ideas between the sentences of John. This he did throughout the Bible, and, in the minds of many unwary people, Scofield's ideas are equated with the Word of God itself.

Had Scofield put his Notes in separate books rather than inserting them inside the Bible itself, there seems to be little doubt that his books would have joined those of Darby's in gathering dust and not being reprinted. The best evidence of this fact lies in the great dearth of information about the man himself in our libraries today, while his reference Bible is a household word. Only his being associated with Paul and Peter, through his audacity in placing his personal ideas on the same sacred pages as theirs, has kept his name alive. And in the minds of some of Scofield's devoted followers, to differ from him is tantamount to differing from Paul or Peter! The following quotation bears mute testimony:

> One young minister I know, pastor of a large church, has been driven almost frantic by constant persecution day in and day out. He is an able, orthodox preacher with a distinctly prophetic note in his teaching. Because he does not preach dispensationalism, his congregation will acknowledge no good in him. He has repeatedly been driven to the point of resigning and taking another church, but feels it his duty to save this church for the Christian faith (W. D. Chamberlain, *The Church Faces the Isms*, pp. 106, 107).

The *Scofield Bible* has done good at points where it has dealt with the cardinal doctrines of historic Christianity. Scofield was a conservative Bible believer, and brought his Notes into existence at a time when the Bible was being attacked on many sides by the so-called higher critics and other liberal theologians. Scofield's defense of the major doctrines of the Bible called forth a renewed interest in Bible study at a time when such a challenge was sorely needed. Followers of Scofield also manifest a respect for the authority of Scripture that is sorely lacking in many Christian circles today.

It must be stated, however, that the *Scofield Bible* contains many teachings which are at variance with historic teachings of the Christian church. Many have questioned whether the good done by this man is not overshadowed by these new and dangerous theories.

An advanced Bible student might read the *Scofield Reference Bible* critically and get some good points from it, and at the same time avoid its erroneous doctrines. However, in the hands of a novice or young convert, this can be a dangerous book. Not least among these dangers is the superior attitude it implants in the minds of its readers. No doctrine of the Bible presents the least problem to these Bible "experts." Nor do they need any further study—all they need is contained in the footnotes of the *Scofield Reference Bible.*

.... These good people do not lack faith and zeal, but they sadly lack knowledge; and the tragedy of the situation lies just here, that this is the very thing they think they have obtained from the *Scofield Bible!* They are apt to say in their hearts, and not infrequently with their lips: "I have more understanding than all my teachers—because I have a Scofield Bible" (Albertus Pieters, *A Candid Examination of the Scofield Bible,* p. 5).

From a position of entire ignorance of the Scriptures to a position of oracular religious certainty—especially respecting eschatological matters—for some people requires from three to six months with a *Scofield Bible* (T. T. Shields, *The Gospel Witness* for April 7, 1932).

I readily recognize that the *Scofield Bible* is very popular with novices, that is, those newly come to the faith, and also with many of longer Christian experience who are but superficial students of Scripture. Ready-made clothes are everywhere popular with people of average size . . . On the same principle, ready-made religious ideas will always be popular, especially with those indisposed to the exertion of fitting their religious conceptions to an ever-increasing scriptural knowledge. That common human disposition very largely explains the popularity of the *Scofield Bible* (*ibid.*).

In the field of Systematic Theology he is good, for there he utilizes the fruits of the standard Protestant and Calvinistic thinking; but in general Bible knowledge he makes many mistakes, and in his eschatology he goes far astray from anything the church has ever believed. Undoubtedly this oracular and authoritative manner has been effective, but it is not to be excused for that reason. It seems like a harsh judgment, but in the interest of truth it must be uttered: Dr. Scofield in this was acting the part of an intellectual charlatan, a fraud who pretends to knowledge which he does not possess; like a quack doctor, who is ready with a confident diagnosis in many cases where a competent physician is unable to decide (Pieters, *op. cit.*).

Scofield's worst critics are men who have come out of his camp, and who remain true to the Bible as the infallible Word of God. A list of these men would include such outstanding men as Mauro, Gordon, G. Campbell Morgan, and Harry Rimmer. Paul B. Fischer, himself a graduate of Wheaton, wrote a pamphlet entitled *Ultra Dispensationalism is Modernism.* Fischer attacks dispensationalism as being a twin to liberalism on two points: (1) the deity of Christ, and (2) the disunity of the Bible.

In 1954 a committee of nine men headed by E. Schuyler English was formed to revise the Scofield Bible. They hope to finish their work by 1963.

A great need exists for the followers of C. I. Scofield to consider objectively the fact that so many earnest, conservative students of the Bible have left his school of theological thought. These sincere Christians need to become concerned over the divisions caused among conservative men of God by the footnotes and other personal insertions Dr. Scofield added to the King James Version of the Holy Bible. It would be well for these folk to realize that any sincere man, including Scofield, can be sincerely wrong.

It is well to keep in mind, too, that we conservatives are not divided over the Bible; we are divided, rather, over the personal explanations which a *man* took the liberty of inserting alongside the inspired writings of the Bible. The gist of the entire controversy at this point, it seems to me, lies in the fact that many of Scofield's most devoted disciples equate his Notes with the inspired words of the writers of the New Testament. The difficulty arises when they attempt to force this equation upon the minds and hearts of others.

We will continue to have tensions until this man is recognized as an extracanonical writer and his ideas are brought into the theological arena, where his good points may be accepted gratefully while his mistaken ideas may be discarded without fear of reprisal.

Having once been a devoted disciple of Scofield, this writer knows the difficulty of becoming objective after years of being subjective to, and captivated by, his great legal mind.

Scofield was, no doubt, an outstanding man. He was, however, *only* a man; and neither he nor his footnotes were infallible.

IV

DISPENSATIONALIST BELIEFS—SALVATION

Dispensationalists derive their name from their teaching that the entire program of God is divided into seven dispensations. Five of these have passed into history, we are living in the sixth, and the seventh dispensation will be an earthly reign of one thousand years (the millennium) following the rapture of the church. Although the word "dispensational" literally means a stewardship or type of economy, they take it to designate a given *period of time* during which God works in a distinct manner with mankind.

The *Scofield Bible* (page 5, notes 4, 5) deals with the seven dispensations of their system. They are innocency, conscience, human government, promise, law, grace, and kingdom. According to Scofield, each of these dispensations begins a new and distinct method of testing mankind and each ends in man's failure and judgment. One of the main emphases of dispensational thought is that they insist that each of these seven dispensations has its peculiar system of testing; and obedience to the existing method brings the approval of God upon the individual or nation being tested.

Although dispensationalists deny the charge, it has been said that these alleged seven distinct manners of testing create seven different plans of salvation. Certainly Cyrus Ingerson Scofield carried water on both shoulders at this point, saying in some places that all people are saved in the same manner, but indicating in others that salvation was gained in a different manner during each of the seven periods. An example of his dual plans of salvation is found in the *Scofield Bible* (page 1115, note 2) where he is contrasting the dispensation of law with that of grace. "The point of testing is *no longer* legal obedience *as the condition of salvation*, but acceptance or rejection of Christ . . ." It is difficult to interpret this statement in any other way than that he was saying folk under the law were saved by *one* "condition" while we under grace are saved by *another* "condition." His words, "no longer," indicate that there was a time when legal obedience *was* the means of salvation!

Lewis Sperry Chafer, another prominent leader among the dispensationalists, also—in his insistence on a complete isolation of

the New Testament dispensation from that of the Old Testament—
actually teaches two different plans of salvation. Writing in *Dispensationalism* (p. 416), he makes the following statement:

> The essential elements of a grace administration—faith as the
> sole basis of acceptance with God, unmerited acceptance through a
> perfect standing in Christ, the present possession of eternal life, an
> absolute security from all condemnation, and the enabling power
> of the indwelling Spirit—*are not found in the kingdom administration.*
> On the other hand, it is declared to be the fulfilling of "the law and
> the prophets" (Matt. 5:17, 18; 7:12), and is seen to be an extension
> of the Mosaic Law into realms of meritorious obligation . . (italics
> mine).

When this paragraph by Chafer is broken down into its com-
ponent parts, the following points can be distinguished clearly: (1)
he gives the characteristics, including "faith as the sole basis of acceptance with God," of the present "dispensation"; (2) he says the
alleged coming "dispensation" (millennium) will operate under a
different plan, since none of the above mentioned characteristics
(note that this would include the mode of salvation) "are to be
found in the kingdom administration"; (3) he says that the alleged
coming millennial kingdom will be a continuation of the Old
Testament plan, i.e., "it is declared to be the fulfilling of the law
and the prophets."

From these three points a syllogism can be formed easily. The
syllogism would be as follows:

1. In the present dispensation, we have "faith as the sole
basis of acceptance with God . . ."

2. In the coming kingdom administration, this plan will not
be in effect. They "are not found in the kingdom administration."
Since, according to the dispensationalists, people will be saved
during the millennium, they must of necessity be saved in some
other manner than "faith as the sole basis of acceptance with God."

3. Therefore, inasmuch as the coming dispensation will be
"an extension of the Mosaic Law into realms of meritorious obli-
gation," the people under the Mosaic Law also were saved in a
manner different from the present dispensation.

Chafer's argument could also be illustrated in a diagram as
follows:

1	2	3
Old Testament	*"Church Age"*	*"Kingdom Age"*
Salvation by legal obedience	Salvation by grace	Legal obedience
(In effect until the Cross)	alone (Legal obedi-	resumed (On a
	ence postponed)	more perfect
		basis)

In another book (*The Kingdom in History and Prophecy*, p. 70) Chafer again distinguishes between two different modes of salvation:

> In the light of these seven "present truth" realities we are enabled to recognize how great is the effect of the change from "the law which came by Moses" and "grace and truth which came by Jesus Christ." And when these changed, age-long conditions have run their course we are assured that *there will be a return to the legal kingdom grounds* and the exaltation of that nation to whom pertain the covenants and promises (italics mine).

It should be noted, in view of the above statement, that if there is to be a return to a certain means of salvation, then another means of salvation must of necessity be in operation at the present time.

In the writings of another dispensationalist we also note a reference to more than one plan of salvation based upon a distinct separation of the so-called dispensations. William Evans (*Outline Studys of the Bible*, p. 34) says:

> This is sometimes called the Age of the Church, or the Church period. The characteristic of this age is that *salvation is no longer by legal obedience*, but by the personal acceptance of the finished work of Jesus Christ, who by his meritorious ministry has procured for us a righteousness of God" (italics mine).

Evans clearly states that during this present age salvation is through personal acceptance of the meritorious ministry (the cross) of Christ, while in the age preceding this one, people were saved by legal obedience. If words have any meaning at all, then this dispensationalist—who is merely being consistent with dispensationalist teachings—has presented two clear and distinct means of salvation, one by legal obedience and the other by the cross of Christ.

That thinking people have taken dispensationalism to present various means of salvation is evident in the report adopted by the Southern Presbyterian Church in the United States. That report, adopted by this assembly in May, 1944, was in part as follows:

It is the unanimous opinion of your Committee that Dispensation-alism is out of accord with the system of the doctrines set forth in the Confession of Faith, not primarily or simply in the field of eschatology, but because it attacks the very heart of the theology of our Church. Dispensationalism rejects the doctrine that God has, since the Fall, but one plan of salvation for all mankind and affirms that God has been through the ages administering various and diverse plans of salvation for various groups. . . .

In a further effort to portray distinct groups being dealt with in distinct ways in given periods of time, dispensationalists teach that there are four gospels to be preached (some have already been preached, and one is being preached in the present age) according to God's plan. Each of these is said to be for a given period of time and great pains are taken to establish the fact that each of these gospels is different from the other three. These four gospels are described on page 1343 of the *Scofield Reference Bible*. The follow-ing is a paraphrased description as given by C. I. Scofield:

1. *The gospel of the kingdom.* This is the preaching of the good news that God had promised to set up an earthly kingdom. This kingdom was to be political, spiritual, Israelitish, universal; and was to be ruled over by Jesus as the greater Son of David. It was to last one thousand years.

2. *The gospel of the grace of God.* This is the good news that Jesus died, was buried, and that he rose again. Scofield says that one of the main characteristics of this gospel is that it saves "wholly apart from forms and ordinances," the plain implication being that this is not true of some of the other three gospels.

3. *The everlasting gospel.* This is to be preached by Jews after the church is raptured, but before the beginning of the millennium. Scofield says of this gospel that it is neither the gospel of the king-dom, nor of grace. It is the good news that those who were saved during the "great tribulation" will enter the millennial reign.

4. *That which Paul calls "my gospel."* This is the gospel of grace, but has a fuller development than that preached by Christ and the apostles! Paul has been given new insight into the "mys-tery" of the church and this is included in "Paul's gospel."

According to this theory of four gospels, the first of them was preached by John the Baptist and by our Lord, until the proffered kingdom was rejected by the Jews and had to be postponed while the church age was ushered in by the death of our Lord on the cross.

After his plan to establish a kingdom was frustrated by the Jews, our Lord changed to the second form of the gospel and began to preach that he would be crucified, buried, and resurrected. This gospel was preached by our Lord during the remainder of his ministry and then by the apostles until the time of Paul.

Upon receiving a fuller revelation concerning the church, which neither Jesus nor any of the other apostles had been permitted to disclose, Paul began to preach number four of the distinctive gospels held by dispensationalism. In other words, what Paul termed "my gospel" was quite an improvement over that preached by our Lord. This is the same gospel, according to this theory, that we are supposed to preach today. Note, we are not to preach the gospel preached by our Lord, but that which was preached by Paul.

Number three of these gospels will not be preached until after the present "church age" is ended and the church has been taken out of the world. Then, after the "everlasting gospel" has been preached and the millennium established, Jewish converts will begin to preach the "gospel of the kingdom" again. Note that this gospel of the kingdom is the first gospel preached by our Lord, which gospel was rejected and then postponed. Whereas our Lord failed in his presentation of it, the Jewish nation is going to succeed!

In view of the fact that this theory holds to four distinct gospels—each having its own characteristics differing from the others—and in view of the fact that each one is said to bring about salvation, it is difficult indeed to escape a doctrine of four plans of salvation. And this, according to the New Testament, amounts to heresy.

V

DISPENSATIONALIST BELIEFS—THE SCRIPTURES

In keeping with dispensationalist views on the completely separate dispensations, the Scriptures are said to have been given *dispensationally*, i.e., different passages of the Bible are directed to different dispensations. Unless one interprets each passage of Scripture dispensationally, one is in a hopeless quandary and can never expect to understand the Bible. Scofield (*What Do the Prophets Say?*, p. 9) offered II Peter 1:20 as a proof-text for this method of interpretation. Having quoted the verse, Scofield went on to say, "That is, no prophecy is to be interpreted by itself, but in harmony with the whole body of prediction on any given subject."

An examination of the verse in question will reveal that the interpretation placed on it by Scofield is equally as arbitrary as his so-called dispensations. "Knowing this first, that no prophecy of scripture is of private interpretation. For no prophecy ever came by the will of man: but men spake from God, being moved by the Holy Spirit" (II Peter 1:20, 21). When the verse is examined in its setting it is soon discovered that Peter was not even speaking of how Scripture should be *interpreted*, but rather he was speaking of how prophecy was *given*. Whereas Scofield has Peter saying that "no prophecy is to be interpreted privately," what Peter actually said was that "no prophet wrote down his own private interpretations, but that he (the prophet) spoke only what the Holy Spirit moved him to write." Peter said this to indicate the *authority* of the Bible, not its interpretation.

Dispensationalists not only divide the Scriptures into seven compartments with relation to time, they also divide them according to the people being dealt with. They say that the Bible itself divides mankind into three distinct groups and then proceeds to address these groups separately. This theory is based on I Corinthians 10:32 alone. One verse of scripture, they say, may be addressed by the Holy Spirit to Gentiles, while the very next verse may be addressing Jews. It can readily be seen how difficult it is to "rightly divide the Word of Truth" dispensationally. In order to gain a correct understanding one would need to take all the individual verses of the Bible and assign each verse to one of three categories—Jew, Gentile, or Christian. If this be the correct method of dividing the Word, then someone could perform a genuine service by publishing the Bible in three separate sections! Dispensationalists, in effect, do so divide the Bible. Chafer (*Dispensationalism*, p. 34) teaches that the only scriptures addressed specifically to Christians are the Gospel of John (especially the upper room discourse), the book of Acts, and the Epistles!

Obviously, this arbitrary and reckless division of the Bible into three compartments is an attempt to minimize the place of the church and to elevate the place of national Israel in the Bible. One example of how they take passages historically attributed to the church and assign them to Israel can be seen in a statement by William L. Pettingill (*Bible Questions Answered*, p. 112).

> I have long been convinced, and have taught that the Great Commission of Matthew 28:19,20 is primarily applicable to the Kingdom rather than to the Church . . . The Matthew commission will come into force for the Jewish Remnant after the Church is caught away.

Pettingill was an ardent defender of the *Scofield Bible*, and served as dean of the Bible school in Philadelphia, which was founded and presided over by C. I. Scofield himself. This group also taught that Christians ought not pray the Lord's Prayer, since it was a Jewish prayer and was to be prayed by Jews in a later age.

Dispensationalists boast of *literal interpretation of Scripture*, and cast aspersions at those who "spiritualize" some passages of the Bible. Charles C. Ryrie, President of The Philadelphia College of the Bible, says: (*Bibliotheca Sacra*, Vol. 114, July, 1957, p. 254), ". . . only dispensationalism provides the key to *consistent literalism*" (italics mine).

Writing in *Bibliotheca Sacra* (Vol. 113, number 449, January, 1956, p. 4), John F. Walvoord deals with the rapture mentioned in I Thessalonians 4:16, and he contends that it is doubtful whether the Old Testament saints will be raised at that time. He goes on to say, "The tendency of followers of Darby to spiritualize the resurrection of Daniel 12:1-2 as merely the restoration of Israel, thereby refuting its post-tribulationism, is to forsake literal interpretation to gain a point, a rather costly concession for premillenarians who build upon literal interpretation of prophecy."

Here Walvoord makes two admissions: (1) *many dispensationalists do spiritualize* when it is convenient for them to do so; (2) dispensationalists, as a rule, build upon a literal interpretation of *all* prophecy, with men like Walvoord making no allowances at any point.

This is, of course, one of the many dilemmas in which the dispensationalist or Darbyite finds himself in dealing with prophecy. Either he must admit that some prophecies are to be taken in a spiritual manner, as Walvoord said many of his school are doing with Daniel 12:1, 2, or else he must say, with Walvoord, that there are no exceptions, but that all are to be taken literally.

Now, let us see where this latter alternative leads the dispensationalist. In the Old Testament, where they spend most of their time, the Darbyites cannot arbitrarily say: "Oh, but that passage was to the church, while this other one is to the Israelites." They can do this arbitrary maneuvering in the New Testament, but they have narrowed their own field in the Old Testament by insisting that the Christian church is not alluded to therein.

Isaiah prophesied that the mountains shall sing and the trees clap their hands (Isaiah 55:12). It this to be taken *literally?* In Micah 6:1 God invites his people to carry on a conversation with a mountain. Literally? In Joel 3:18 a prophecy is recorded in which God states that "the mountains shall drop down sweet wine, and the hills shall flow with milk." Must this be taken *literally*, or was the Lord speaking figuratively? In Hosea 2:18 God says that he will some day make a covenant for his people between the beasts of the fields, with the fowl of heaven, and with the creeping things of the ground. Will this *literally* happen?

Daniel predicted that the destruction of Jerusalem in A.D. 70 would be accomplished by a *flood* (Daniel 9:26). This did not happen literally. Was Daniel mistaken? Or did he not rather speak *spiritually* or figuratively and mean that the city would be flooded with the soldiers of Titus? This latter alternative did happen. The literal interpretation insisted upon by Walvoord would make the biblical account untrue!

Coming to the New Testament the strict dispensationalist still insists upon literal interpretations for each and every passage concerning Israel. Zechariah prophesied that Christ would stand on two mountains (Mount Olivet being divided in two).

> And his feet shall stand in that day upon the Mount of Olives, which is before Jerusalem on the east; and the Mount of Olives shall be cleft in the midst thereof toward the east and toward the west, and there shall be a very great valley; and half of the mountain shall

remove toward the north, and half of it toward the south (Zechariah 14:4).

Surely this could not be the "same Jesus" who was seen ascending up to heaven as recorded in Acts 1:11 and of whom it was said that "this same Jesus" would come in like manner as he was seen to go away. The body that our Lord had then would not be large enough to span two mountains. Now this is not an attempt to be facetious, and it is agreed by all that God is capable of giving Christ a body large enough to span two mountains with one foot resting on each mountain. Yes, this is possible, but it does not seem likely that God will make such a drastic change. And if the dispensationalist hastens to say that these passages are speaking of spiritual things, then he destroys his own argument.

A thoroughly literal interpretation of Scripture is impossible. To quote Dr. Allis:

> The language of the Bible often contains figures of speech. This is especially true of its poetry. In Exodus XIV: 21 Moses declares that the Lord caused the sea to go back by reason of a "strong east wind." In his song of triumph Moses exultantly declares: "and with the blast of thy nostrils the waters were gathered together" (XV:8). In XIX:4, on the other hand, the Lord reminds Israel through Moses: "I bare you on eagle's wings, and brought you unto myself." No one with any real reverence for Scripture or adequate understanding of its teachings as a whole, would dream of taking either of the last two statements literally. In the poetry of Psalms, in the elevated style of prophecy, and even in simple historical narration, figures of speech appear which obviously are not meant to be and cannot be understood literally.

> The great theme of the Bible is God, and His redemptive dealings with mankind. God is a spirit; and these spiritual and heavenly realities are often set forth under the form of earthly objects and human relationships. When Jesus said, "Ye must be born again," He was not referring to a physical but a spiritual birth. When He said, "Destroy this temple," He meant His body. When He said, "He that eateth my flesh and drinketh my blood, hath everlasting life," He was speaking of a spiritual relationship in terms of the Old Testament type. Jesus' Jewish hearers, being literalists, either failed to understand or misunderstood His words. Whether the figurative or "spiritual" interpretation of a given passage is justified or not depends solely upon whether it gives the true meaning. If it is used to empty words of their plain and obvious meaning, to read out of them what is clearly intended by them, then allegorizing or spiritualizing is a term of reproach which is well merited. On the other hand, we should remember the saying of the apostle, that spiritual things are "spiritually discerned." And spiritual

things are more real and more precious than visible, tangible, ephemeral things (Oswald T. Allis, *Prophecy and the Church*, pp. 17, 18)

and as Barrows has well said:

> The youthful student of Scripture should be reminded, first of all, that its figurative language is no less certain and truthful than its plain and literal declarations. The figures of the Bible are employed not simply to please the imagination and excite the feelings, but to teach eternal verities (E. P. Barrows, Companion to the Bible, p. 557).

As one studies the Scriptures and tries to "rightly divide the Word of Truth," it seems evident that the following conclusions must be arrived at concerning the covenants and prophecies of God with his people:

Some were meant to be *literal*, others were meant to be *spiritual;* some were meant to be historical, others to be *eschatological;* some were addressed to *natural descendants* (national Israel), others were addressed to *spiritual descendants* (all believers; compare Gal. 6:16). Our difficulties arise when students of the Bible (oftentimes sincerely) attempt to force a literal meaning into a spiritual prophecy, or an eschatological interpretation into a prediction which has been historically fulfilled already, or when they try to apply spiritual promises to natural Israelites to the exclusion of other nations.

It is theological pandemonium to attempt to take an "either-or" approach to all scriptures. One must recognize both literal and spiritual descendants. Only then will one "rightly divide the Word of Truth." To be sure, this requires intellectual honesty; and all of us should admit that we are not unequivocally certain on every point as to which is meant.

Although hyperliteralism is one of the basic teachings of dispensationalists, they by no means hold a monopoly on it. Many groups within the Christian faith have resorted to a hyperliteral interpretation of Scripture in order to gain their point.

We can best critize the literalists by saying that none really exist! Their greatest inconsistency lies in the fact that all of them at one time or another interpret some passages of the Bible in a figurative or spiritual manner. Let us begin with the leader himself. John Nelson Darby, who founded modern dispensationalism upon a so-called literal interpretation of the Bible, has left us the following statement, made while he was at the height of his popularity as one who interpreted the Scriptures (especially prophecy) *literally.*

> The resurrection (in Daniel 12:2) applies to the Jews . . . *It is a figurative resurrection* of the people, buried as a nation among the Gentiles. In this revival it is said of those who rise: "Some to shame and everlasting contempt." This is what will happen to the Jews. Of those brought out from among the nations, some will enjoy eternal life, but some shall be subject to shame and everlasting contempt (*The Hopes of the Church of God*, p. 138, italics mine).

Let us look at another outstanding "literalist" and just see how literal he really is. Oswald J. Smith, a Presbyterian pastor in Canada, is a world leader among dispensationalists. He is a prolific writer and lecturer on the subject. Smith says (*When the King Comes Back*, p. 31) in speaking of the Scripture writers: "Nor are we going to dishonor God by spiritualizing their utterances. *We take them just as they read*" (italics mine). Now his plain inference is that all who spiritualize passages of scripture dishonor God; and he states that he would be guilty of no such sin. The observant reader does not need to read far in this same book until, alas, the author contradicts himself and "dishonors God" grievously. For on page 50 he says: "Always, everywhere, the BRANCH is Jesus Christ." Is this how Smith "takes the Scriptures *just as they read?*" Why did not the prophets simply say "Jesus" instead of "Branch"? Or else why did Smith not take the prophets' words just as they were uttered? In order to have the Branch refer to Jesus, he must violate his own strict rule of literal interpretation. As the observant reader continues in this same book (p. 65 for example), he discovers that the author takes yet other liberties with the Scriptures, thereby violating his rule of literal interpretation; for on page 65 he says: "A mountain in prophecy is a kingdom." Is this literalism? It is from the pen of this leading spokesman for the school of literal interpretation. By taking the Scriptures "just as they read," this man derives the word "kingdom" from the word "mountain." And from the word "Branch" he derives the word "Jesus"!

Charles C. Ryrie is another dispensationalist who castigates other Christians for "spiritualizing" Scripture, but then takes the same liberties himself as the occasion arises. He says (*The Basis of the Premillennial Faith*, p. 35): "The system of spiritualizing Scripture is a tacit denial of the doctrine of the verbal, plenary inspiration of the Scriptures which this author holds." Note that this blanket statement demands literal interpretation of *all* Scripture. Ryrie shows his inconsistencies on this dictum of literalism at many points in this same book. In chapter 3, on his rules of hermeneutics, he says: "The *figures* for which the *figurative language* stand have a literal fulfillment." He speaks also of the *special principles of interpretation* used by premillennialists in interpreting prophecy. In speaking of interpretation versus application, he says (page 42) "Literal interpretation allows wide latitude in making *spiritual applications* from all passages . . ." On this same page this avowed "literalist" says: "Although much of prophecy is given in plain terms, *much of it is in figurative language*, and constitutes a problem of interpretation." He goes on to say that there are *different ways to apply this figurative language.* "The use of types (by premillennialists) is perfectly legitimate as illustration of the truth though they should not be used to teach doctrine" (p. 43). Then, on page 44, Ryrie says: "In conclusion it may be stated that in connection with the use of *figurative language, the interpreter should not look for the literal sense of the words* employed in *the figure*, but for the *literal sense intended* by the *use of the figure*" (all italics mine). It is amusing indeed to have read, just a few pages before, that this man called any and all "spiritualizing" a tacit denial of the Bible. Then he goes on to say that it is necessary for his school of thought to devise "special principles of interpretation," to determine when a doctrine is involved in a given passage, and even to decide what was "intended" by each given writer's language. This is literalism?

Examples could be heaped upon one another showing outstanding dispensationalists, like those mentioned above, who violate their own dictum of literalism. However, one last example must suffice at this time. On page 1009 of the *Scofield Bible* (note 1) we have a glaring example of the liberties taken in interpretation. The footnote has to do with chapter 10 of Matthew's Gospel. That this entire chapter was addressed specifically to the twelve disciples there can be no argument. Chapter 10 begins with these words: "And when he had called unto him his twelve disciples . . ." Having called these disciples unto himself, our Lord gave them instructions for their personal ministry. Then, to prove to ourselves that the entire chapter was addressed to these twelve, chapter 11 begins with the words: "And it came to pass, when Jesus had made an end of commanding his twelve disciples . . ." So that, throughout chapter 10, Jesus is addressing his remarks to his twelve disciples. Scofield, however, as is typical of his entire collection of footnotes, looks into the mind of Jesus and sees there many meanings which were not recorded anywhere in the Bible! For Scofield tells his readers that verses 16-23 of this tenth chapter of Matthew reach far beyond the personal ministry of the twelve disciples, covering the sphere of our present age. And whereas Jesus, in verse 23, said specifically to his twelve apostles "when they persecute *you* . . . *Ye* shall not have gone over the cities of Israel until I shall join *you* . . .," Scofield says of this verse that Jesus really had in view the preaching ministry of a remnant of Jews who would be preaching during a time of tribulation *after the church is raptured.* And whereas the average reader would gain the impression that Jesus was saying (in Matthew 10:23) that he would join his twelve apostles before their ministry had covered all the cities of Israel, Scofield informs his readers that this did not even refer to the ministry of those twelve—whom a literal reading would have Jesus addressing—but that it really refers to a group of Jews who will be preaching a different gospel after this present gospel period has closed. And all of this is by the pen of a man who has done more, perhaps, than any other individual, to impress upon people that the Bible should be taken *literally,* "just as it reads"!

VI

DISPENSATIONALIST BELIEFS—
ISRAEL AND THE KINGDOM OF GOD

According to dispensationalists, God has two distinct bodies of people with whom he is working: Israel and the church. There is a separate plan for each of these two peoples. Israel is said to be an earthly people, while the church represents a heavenly body. National Israel's expectation is an earthly kingdom; the church's hope is eternal bliss in heaven. While the church realized her goal through belief in the finished work of Christ on the cross, Israel's goal will finally be realized through legal obedience.

Whereas historic Christianity has held that the purpose of our Lord's first advent was to die on the cross for the sins of the whole world, the dispensationalist teaches that his real purpose was to establish an earthly kingdom. This, they say, was to have been an earthly, political kingdom over which Christ would have ruled from the literal throne of David, and in which all Old Testament prophecies were to be *literally* fulfilled. That is to say that children would have played with ferocious animals, lions would have eaten hay while oxen ate lion's food, and Jesus would have ruled over all with a rod of iron. This kingdom would have been a perfected continuation of the Davidic kingdom of the Old Testament with David's greater Son, Jesus, ruling in his place for one thousand years.

Before continuing in a further description of dispensational teaching with reference to this alleged earthly kingdom, we should like to state that this teaching (that Christ aspires to sit on the literal throne of David) is one of the many evidences of the weak Christology in the dispensational system. Even if God should resurrect the throne on which David sat, which throne has long since decayed and turned to dust, it would indeed be a demotion of the lowest order for our Lord, who occupies the throne of heaven, to be a successor to a throne once occupied by an earthly king! And yet this is one of the very highpoints in dispensational eschatology. Jesus, they say, failed once to sit on the throne of David, but at the second advent he is to have that high honor! Our Lord has for nearly two thousand years occupied the throne of which David's throne was a mere type. Peter depicts this in Acts 2:29-36.

To return now to the dispensational teaching about the kingdom for Israel, they teach that Jesus came to earth the first time fully intending to establish an earthly millennial kingdom with his chosen people, Israel.

Clarence Larkin (*Rightly Dividing the Word*, p. 51), in describing the ministry of John the Baptist as a forerunner to Christ, said: "Prepare the way of the Lord for what? Not for the Cross but for the Kingdom."

M. R. DeHaan, well-known radio preacher, made the following statement with reference to the first advent of our Lord (*The Second Coming of Jesus*, p. 98):

> . . . the kingdom of heaven is the reign of heaven's King on earth. This Jesus offered to the nation of Israel when he came the first time, but they rejected it and he went to the cross.

W. E. Blackstone (*Jesus is Coming*, p. 46), who is said to share the honor with C. I. Scofield as one of those who did most to perpetuate dispensationalism in this country, said concerning the first advent: "He would have set up the kingdom, but they rejected and crucified Him."

On page 998 of the *Scofield Bible* we read that, when Christ appeared the first time on earth to the Jewish people, the next order of revelation as it then stood should have been the setting up of the Davidic kingdom.

Lewis Sperry Chafer (*Systematic Theology*) said:

> The kingdom was announced by John the Baptist, Christ and the apostles. The Gospel of the Kingdom (Matt. 4:23; 9:35) and the proclamation that the kingdom of heaven was at hand (Matt. 3:2; 4:17; 10:7) consisted of a legitimate offer to Israel of the promised *earthly* Davidic kingdom, designed particularly for Israel. However, the Jewish nation rejected their King and with him the Kingdom (Quoted from George Ladd, *Crucial Questions About the Kingdom of God*, p. 50).

Why did the Christ fail in his attempt to establish a kingdom during his first advent? Dispensationalists say it was because his success depended on the consent of the Jewish nation. S. D. Gordon (*Quiet Talks About Jesus*, p. 131) says: "Everything must be done through man's consent." Commenting further on this he said (sec. IV):

> God proposes, man disposes. God proposed a king, and a world-wide kingdom with great prosperity and peace. Man disposed of that plan, for the bit of time and space controlled by his will.

The question immediately arises in our minds: If the Jews were able to frustrate God's plan at the first advent of our Lord, then what assurance have we that his second advent will not also somehow be thwarted? We say this rather facetiously, but the fact still remains that our *hope* of the second coming is built on the *success* of his first advent. "Our hope is built on nothing less than Jesus' blood and righteousness."

When the Jews rejected Christ's legitimate offer of the kingdom, say the dispensationalists, that kingdom was then postponed until the second coming of Christ. Then the same earthly Davidic kingdom which they are supposed to have refused will be established in the form of the millennium. During the millennium all the plans which were supposedly thwarted by the Jews at the first advent will be carried out in a literal manner.

The importance played in dispensational theology by the alleged kingdom which was offered, rejected, and postponed until the millennium, can be seen in the following lengthy doctrinal statement:

> The Magnum Opus of dispensational eschatology will be found in Lewis Sperry Chafer's *Systematic Theology*, where the entire range of theology is interpreted in the light of dispensational eschatology. From this work we extract the following interpretation of the kingdom of God.
>
> Two specific realms must be considered: The kingdom of God, which includes all intelligences in heaven or on earth who are willingly subject to God, and the kingdom of heaven, which is the manifestation of the kingdom of God at any time in its earthly form. Thus the kingdom of God appears on earth in various forms or embodiments during the centuries.
>
> 1. There was first of all the kingdom in the Old Testament theocracy in which God ruled over Israel in and through the judges.
>
> 2. The kingdom was covenanted by God as he entered into unconditional covenant with David and gave to Israel its national hope of a permanent earthly kingdom (II Samuel 7).
>
> 3. The kingdom was predicted by the prophets as a glorious kingdom for Israel on earth when the Messianic Son of David would sit on David's throne and rule over the nations from Jerusalem.

4. The kingdom was announced by John the Baptist, Christ, and the apostles. The Gospel of the kingdom (Matt. 4:23; 9:35) and the proclamation that the kingdom of heaven was at hand (Matt. 3:2; 4:17; 10:7) consisted of a legitimate offer to Israel of the promised earthly Davidic kingdom, designed particularly for Israel. However, the Jewish nation rejected their king and with Him, the kingdom.

5. Because of Israel's rejection, the kingdom was postponed until the second advent of Christ. The millennial kingdom was offered, and postponed; but it will be instituted on earth after Christ's return. Since the kingdom was postponed it is a great error to attempt, as is so commonly done, to build a kingdom on the first advent of Christ as its basis, for, according to the Scriptures, the kingdom which was offered to Israel was rejected and is therefore delayed, to be realized only with the second advent of Christ.

6. The kingdom, because it was rejected and postponed, entered a mystery form (Matt. 13) for the present age. This mystery form of the kingdom has to do with the Church age when the kingdom of heaven is embodied in Christendom. God is now ruling on the earth insofar as the parables of the mystery of the kingdom of heaven require. In this mystery phase of the kingdom, good and evil mingle together and are to grow together until Christ returns.

7. The kingdom is to be reannounced by a Jewish remnant of 144,000 in final anticipation of Messiah's return. At the beginning of the great tribulation, which occurs immediately before the return of Christ, the Church will be raptured, taken out of the world, to be with Christ. An election of Israel is then sealed by God to proclaim throughout all the world the Gospel of the kingdom (Matt 24:14), i.e., that the Davidic kingdom, the kingdom of heaven, is about to be set up.

8. The millennial kingdom will then be realized as Christ returns in power and glory at the conclusion of the tribulation. Then Israel, which has been gathered from its dispersion through the earth to Messiah, will accept Him as such, and will enter the millennial kingdom as the covenanted people (George E. Ladd, *Crucial Questions About the Kingdom of God*, pp. 50,51).

Noting again that dispensationalists teach the kingdom to have been offered, rejected, and postponed until a later age, we pose the question: *What if the Jews had accepted Jesus' offer to establish an earthly Davidic kingdom at his first advent?* According to dispensationalist teaching, people would then have been saved by legal obedience. In the light of this fact, dispensationalism would also teach—when carried to its logical conclusion—that the cross would not have been necessary as a means of salvation.

Let the dispensationalists themselves speak at this point. S. D. Gordon (*Quiet Talks About Jesus*, p. 114) says:

> It can be said at once that His dying was not God's own plan. It was conceived somewhere else and yielded to by God. God has a plan of atonement by which men who were willing could be saved from sin and its effect.
>
> That plan is given in the Old Hebrew code. To the tabernacle or temple, under prescribed regulations, a man could bring some animal which he owned. The man brought that which was his own. It represented him.

In the above statement a dispensationalist has been consistent at least. If, as he says, God offered a plan other than the cross, and if men had accepted that plan, then they would have been saved thereby. Since the proffered kingdom was alleged to have been an Old Testament kingdom then men would have abided by Old Testament sacrifices. It needs to be said here, however, that the Old Testament sacrifices were never intended as a method of salvation. They pointed to the Lamb of God who took away the sins of the world. The Scriptures plainly teach that the "blood of bulls and goats" could not bring about salvation, but that they were a type of the cross of Calvary.

What if that legal kingdom had been accepted? Let Lewis Sperry Chafer answer (*The Kingdom in History and Prophecy*, p. 56): "It was a bona fide offer and, had they received him as their king, *the nation's hopes would have been realized*" (italics mine).

Dispensationalists make two assertions concerning the kingdom: (1) The kingdom of heaven is Messianic, mediatorial, and Davidic (Scofield's footnote, p. 1003); it also signifies the Messianic earth rule of Jesus Christ, the Son of David (footnote p. 996). (2) Although there is a present kingdom in the world, this is the kingdom of God and is not the same as the kingdom of heaven. Now here hangs the entire dispensational position. They look for a *future* Davidic kingdom, i.e., a future millennium, based on an alleged distinction between the kingdom of heaven and the kingdom of God. If the fact can be scripturally established that the kingdom of heaven is *synonymous* with the kingdom of God— which the dispensationalist admits is present already—then two things are true: (1) the Davidic kingdom has already been established, and (2) there will be no future millennium, but it too began at the first advent. This we believe the Bible teaches.

In Matthew's Gospel we have the inspired record of our Lord's teaching concerning John the Baptist. He clearly states that John preached a kingdom message following the time of the law and the prophets.

> And from the days of John the Baptist until now *the kingdom of heaven suffereth violence*, and men of violence take it by force. For all the prophets and the law prophesied unto John (Matt. 11:12, 13).

We should note two things about the above statement: (1) the content of John's message is called by our Lord "the kingdom of heaven," (2) in order to suffer violence a thing must be in existence; so that the kingdom existed already during the earthly ministry of John.

Luke also records a conversation of our Lord during which He spoke of John the Baptist in these words:

> The law and the prophets were until John: from that time *the gospel of the kingdom of God is preached*, and every man entereth violently into it (Luke 16:16).

These could well have been two separate messages delivered by our Lord. The important thing to note is that in both messages he fixed the time as being the same; he said that John took up where the law and the prophets left off and that he preached the gospel of a kingdom. In one message (Matt. 11:12) our Lord referred to that kingdom as "the kingdom of *heaven*," while on the other occasion (Luke 16:16)—in speaking of the same man, same time, and same message—he referred to that same kingdom as "the kingdom of *God*."

Another scriptural evidence that the kingdom of heaven and the kingdom of God are synonymous terms is found in two accounts of the sending out of the Twelve. Two inspired writers, "speaking as they were moved by the Holy Spirit," give the accounts. One of these inspired men chose to use the term "kingdom of heaven," while the other preferred "the kingdom of God." No doubt this difference in wording is owing to the fact that the Gospels were addressed to separate groups. The Jews hesitated to use the name of God, so the one who addressed them would respect this custom and substitute the name "heaven" in place of the name "God." But the important thing for us to consider is the fact that these men could use either term, proving to us that both terms indicated the same reality.

> And as ye go, preach, saying, *The kingdom of heaven* is at hand (Matthew 10:7).

> And he sent them forth to preach *the kingdom of God*, and to heal the sick (Luke 9:2).

Matthew and Luke record the beginning of our Lord's earthly ministry. And, while there can be no doubt that both refer to his opening message, one uses the term "kingdom of heaven," while the other refers to "the kingdom of God." Would dispensationalists have us believe Jesus preached two different kingdoms as being at hand at the same time?

> From that time began Jesus to preach, and to say, *Repent ye;* for *the kingdom of heaven is at hand* (Matthew 4:17).

Compare verse 12 for the time element in Matthew 4:17. Like the following passage, it refers to the time immediately following John's death.

> Now after John was delivered up, Jesus came into Galilee, preaching the gospel of God, and saying, the time is fulfilled, and *the kingdom of God is at hand: repent ye*, and believe the gospel (Mark 1:14, 15).

If further proof be needed to establish the fact that these two terms are synonymous, let us turn to Matthew 19:23, 24. In this passage we have a case of Hebrew parallelism in which our Lord says the same thing twice, for effect. The interesting thing to observe is that our Lord himself, without changing subjects, refers to the same kingdom in two different terms.

> And Jesus said unto his disciples, Verily I say unto you, It is hard for a rich man *to enter the kingdom of heaven*. And again I say unto you, it is easier for a camel to go through a needle's eye, than for a rich man *to enter into the kingdom of God*.

These scriptures show conclusively that the kingdom of heaven and the kingdom of God are one and the same. Therefore, dispensationalists are looking for a future kingdom which in reality has been in existence since the first advent of our Lord. They admit that, *whenever* the Davidic kingdom is set up on the earth, Israel's hope will have been realized; *they also admit that one kingdom of God came into existence with the birth of the Christian church.*

To prove that *the New Testament knows only one kingdom,* called by two different names, is to prove by the dispensationalists' own arguments that the kingdom is a present reality, identical with Christianity. And, since the dispensationalist teaches that the kingdom is to come about during the millennium, his own argument must also lead to the conclusion that the millennium is the inter-advent period. This, we believe, the New Testament clearly teaches. One clear description of the Messianic reign of Christ (the millennium) is recorded in Matthew 11:1-6. It is to be noted that this reign began with our Lord's first advent, not at the second coming.

John Calvin, the great theologian of the Reformation, counted as heresy the idea of an earthly establishment of the Davidic kingdom. The following quotation is from the pen of Heinrich Quistorp (*Calvin's Doctrine of the Last Things,* pp. 123, 158).

> The fact that Christ as the Son of Man will appear on the clouds of heaven is a plain indication that His divine glory and the glory of His kingdom will be no earthly phenomenon, as the disciples had supposed. He who in His incarnate life had hidden His heavenly majesty under the form of a servant will then be manifest with all the tokens of the power of that kingdom which is from heaven because it is the kingdom of God.

> This kingdom of Christ will be an eternal kingdom because it is the kingdom of God. Calvin emphasized this with vigour. Hence he decidedly rejects the chiliasm of the fanatics which would make of the kingdom of Christ a purely temporal and transient one. Calvin sees in chiliasm a deceptive fantasy by means of which Satan began to corrupt the Christian hope soon after apostolic times. "I dismiss the notion that Satan began already in the time of Paul to ruin this hope . . . But shortly afterwards the Chiliasts arose who fixed and narrowed the conception of Christ's kingdom as being of a thousand years duration."

It is a paradox indeed to encounter so many today who claim to be "Calvinistic" following after dispensational teachings, which are in total contradiction to the teachings of Calvin.

VII

DISPENSATIONALIST BELIEFS—THE CHURCH

With reference to the Christian church, dispensationalists believe it came into being as a result of the rejection of the alleged earthly kingdom. They teach that the church was kept hidden in the mind of God until he was ready to establish it. Although Jesus may have hinted at it, they say, it did not actually come into prominence until Paul began to preach "my gospel." Dispensationalists teach that none of the Old Testament and in fact very little of the New Testament deals with the church.

We need to keep before the reader the dispensational belief that Israel and the church are two distinct bodies, that each has its separate plan in God's program, and that each has a different destination. Israel is said to be an earthly covenant people while the church is said to be a heavenly body. After the one-thousand years earthly reign (millennium) the church will be returned to heaven (from whence she will have come in order to reign in the millennium, in a lesser position than that held by Israel) while Israel will remain eternally on the earth. Chafer said (*Dispensationalism*, pp. 40, 41):

> It should be observed that though Judaism and Christianity have much in common, they never merge the one into the other. Having each its own eschatology reaching on into eternity . . . The Word of God distinguishes between earth and heaven, even after they are created new. Similarly and as clearly it distinguishes between God's consistent and eternal earthly purpose, which is the substance of Judaism; and His consistent and eternal heavenly purpose which is the substance of Christianity, and it is as illogical and fanciful to contend that Judaism and Christianity ever merge as it would be to contend that heaven and earth cease to exist as separate spheres.

Oswald T. Allis (*Prophecy and the Church*, p. vi of the Preface) has given a concise distinction between dispensational teaching concerning the church, as opposed to the views of the great majority of Christians:

> According to one view, the Church is the fulfillment of prophecy; according to the other, it interrupts that fulfillment. According to one view the Church age is the "day of salvation"; according to the other view the Church age is only an episode, even if a very important one, in that day of salvation; and the salvation of Israel and of "the enormous majority of mankind" will follow the removal of the Church.

How do dispensationalists maintain this distinction between Israel and the Christian church? They maintain it, to their own satisfaction, by holding to many premises never held by historic Christianity. Chafer makes a correct analysis of this fact in one of his books (*Dispensationalism*, p. 107):

> At the beginning of this thesis it was stated that the doctrinal differences herein discussed are due to the fact that the two schools of interpretation involved stand on widely divergent premises. The dispensationalist believes that throughout the ages God is pursuing two distinct purposes: one related to the earth with earthly people and earthly objectives involved, while the other is related to heaven with heavenly people and heavenly objectives involved, which is Christianity.

Dispensationalists teach that the present "church age" was not revealed to the Old Testament writers. Therefore, the prophets saw the two advents of Christ, but saw nothing intervening between these two comings. These two advents appeared to the prophets as mountain peaks. What they were not permitted to see, however, was that God had a valley (the present dispensation) planned in between these two "peaks." Because this was so, say the dispensationalists, the prophets saw the *two comings* of our Lord blended together as though they were *one*. They go on to say that all prophecies which may *appear to be referring to the first advent* are in reality referring to the second coming. This was one of Darby's "rediscovered truths" which had remained hidden from the great Reformers and all the great writers of Bible commentaries. Darby's "rediscovered truth" on this subject is recorded for us in his book (*The Hopes of the Church of God*, p. 7).

> . . . The greater part of the prophecies, and in a certain sense, we may say all the prophecies, will have their accomplishment at the expiration of the dispensation in which we are.

We have already shown that, according to dispensational teachings, people were offered salvation through the establishment of a millennial kingdom. Had this kingdom been established, the Jewish remnant would have carried out the Great Commission and most of the world's population would have been converted through obedience to the law. The cross then would not have been necessary, according to this teaching. However, the kingdom was not accepted, and so, teach the dispensationalists, it was postponed until the millennium can be set up at the second coming. That postponement has already lasted nearly two thousand years! Now when the kingdom was postponed, its mode of salvation was of course also postponed. It was necessary for God to institute *a temporary mode of salvation* to be in effect during this temporary period. We have said that dispensationalism has separate plans for Israel and the church. Lest this appear to be too sweeping a statement, let us go to the dispensationalists themselves for this teaching.

On page 1011, note 2, of the *Scofield Bible* the author labels the heading: "The new message of Jesus." He has said that our Lord began his ministry with a message of the kingdom, at which time he made an offer to Israel of an earthly kingdom along with salvation by legal obedience. This having been rejected, says Scofield, Jesus began to preach a completely different gospel which now for the first time included a reference to the cross of Calvary. Scofield went on to say, concerning "the new message of Jesus," that our Lord offers "not the kingdom, but rest and service" in his new message.

We have given many quotations to the effect that dispensationalists teach a plan of redemption, other than the cross, offered at the first advent, rejected, and to be renewed during the millennium. If that plan is not in effect today, and if people are being saved, then it stands to reason that they are being saved in some way other than that first offered by Jesus before he began his "new message." The "new way" is the way of the cross, according to dispensationalists.

We quoted S. D. Gordon (*Quiet Talks About Jesus*, p. 114) to the effect that the crucifixion of Jesus was not in God's plan of salvation, but rather that it was "conceived somewhere else," and then "yielded to by God." This, we have said, is the only logical conclusion to be drawn from dispensational teachings. Gordon went on to say (p. 118): "There is no cross in God's plan of atonement." This ties in logically with Scofield's teaching concerning the "new message of Jesus." The first message, they would say, had no cross in it. This the Bible-believing Christian must brand as heresy of the worst sort. The New Testament teaches that the cross was foretold, and that it was foreordained before the foundation of the world. Our Lord, in predicting his death on the cross, said: "For this cause came I into the world."

Chafer (*The Kingdom in History and Prophecy*, p. 51) makes a distinction between the proffered kingdom and the present "dispensation."

It may be concluded that the term "kingdom of heaven" as used in the early ministry of Jesus referred to the Messianic, Davidic, earthly kingdom seen in the Old Testament. As has been noted, the Jewish preachers needed no instruction in the details of that message. It was the hope of their nation, and it was addressed to that nation alone. So, also, an appeal was made with this message for the anticipated national repentance which must precede the setting up of their kingdom in the earth, *and the requirements set forth were legal rather than gracious.* Israel's kingdom was faithfully offered to them by their King at His first appearing (italics mine).

It can be seen from Chafer's remarks that his thesis is, that while our present dispensation has *gracious requirements*, the kingdom offered, rejected, and to be renewed contains *legal requirements*.

J. C. O'Hair, writing in *The Great Blunder of the Church*, said, repeatedly, that there was not a thimble-full of grace in the Synoptic Gospels. This was in line with the teaching that these Gospels were not addressed to Christians but are to take effect in the millennium, under Jews. Chafer said: "At this time (millennium) the King will rule with a rod of iron. *There is no word of the cross or of grace in the kingdom teachings*" (italics mine).

John Nelson Darby is quoted by Oswald T. Allis (*Prophecy and the Church*, p. 76) as follows: "Supposing for a moment that Christ had not been rejected, the kingdom would have been set up on the earth. It could not be so, no doubt, but *it shows the difference between the kingdom and the church*" (italics mine). Darby says plainly here that the difference between the kingdom and the church is that the church needs the cross while the kingdom does not! Chafer (*Dispensationalism*, p. 57) again attempts to show a distinction between the church and Israel. In speaking of eschatology he said:

Judaism has its eschatology *reaching on into eternity* with covenants and promises which are everlasting. On the other hand, Christianity has its eschatology *which is different at every point*. Some of these contrasts are:

1. THE FUTURE OF THIS LIFE. In the case of Israel, the thing to be desired was long life "upon the land, which the Lord thy God giveth thee," whereas the Christian's hope is the prospect of the imminent coming of Christ to take away His Church from the earth (italics mine).

A serious problem arises here, it seems, in the dispensational plan for having Israel spend eternity in an earthly kingdom while

Christians spend eternity in heaven. We refer to the dispensational teaching that Jesus will occupy the throne of David "forever." Now they take this word "forever" always in its most literal sense; this would mean that our Lord could never cease to sit on that throne. Yet the Scriptures teach that a time will come when our Lord will give over the kingdom to the Father and "God will become all in all." How could this be if Jesus were reigning on the throne of David *forever?*

Another facet of dispensational teaching concerning the church is that it is *parenthetic,* and is not the main project at hand. Rather, they say, the church was established by God in order to fill in the *parenthesis* between the time the kingdom was rejected and the time when it will be reinstituted. After the "parenthetic church age" is finished, then God will return to his first love, the Jewish program.

W. R. Newell, (*Romans Verse By Verse,* p. 335) gives the dispensational view on this point:

> When we reflect that, after He has "caught up in the clouds" His Church saints, our Lord is coming back to this earthly people Israel, and will establish them in their land, with a glorious millennial temple and order of worship, to which the Gentile nations must and will submit: then we see that the present time is altogether anomalous! It is a *parenthesis,* in which God is making a "visit" to the Gentiles, to "take out of them a people for His name"; after which, James tells us, our Lord "will Himself return, and build again the tabernacle of David, which is fallen" (Acts 15:16), on Mount Zion, in Jerusalem, where David lived.

Please note that Newell offers no scriptural references for the major portion of this statement; also check the one verse he does use (Acts 15:16) and see that whereas Newell makes it future, James actually said that the scripture had already been fulfilled by the incident at the home of Cornelius!

Dispensationalists consistently quote the words "after this" as being future from James. A more careful reading of the passage, however, will show that James was quoting Amos 9:11 and that the words "after this" are not James' words at all. Rather they are the words which James quotes from Amos. It was Amos, not James, who actually said *that after Amos' time* God would rebuild the tabernacle. James ruled that the account given by Peter (read Acts 15:7-11 for this account) proved that Amos' prophecy on the rebuilding of the "tabernacle" *had been fulfilled in Peter's presence* (Acts 15:14, 15).

This is typical of dispensationalists at this point; rather than producing scriptural proof of their alleged parenthesis, they merely *assume it* in such a matter-of-fact manner that many people never think of questioning it. Chafer offers another example of this sort of reasoning (*Dispensationalism*, p. 34). He begins a long paragraph with the words: "An extensive body of Scripture declares directly or indirectly that the present age is unforseen and intercalary in its character and in it a new humanity appears on the earth with an incomparable new headship in the resurrected Christ, which company is being formed by the regenerating power of the Spirit." We must note here again that, while Chafer refers to an "extensive body of Scripture," he lists not a single verse. Throughout the long paragraph, however, he mentions scriptures on other subjects being dealt with. The present writer has searched dispensational literature in vain for one verse of conclusive scripture dealing with a gap or parenthesis anywhere in God's program.

VIII

THE CHURCH (Continued)

Dispensationalist teaching on the church is one of so many doctrines where the wish is father to the thought; for the Bible simply will not bear out Darby's "rediscovered truth." While much of the New Testament could be used to refute this doctrine, one of Paul's epistles alone will serve to undermine all dispensational teachings concerning the relationship between the church and national Israel.

One might think in terms of dispensationalism versus Paul's letter to the Ephesians:

I. DISPENSATIONAL TEACHING: The church is a parenthesis, i.e., a temporary thing lying between God's two dealings with national Israel.

PAUL'S EPHESIAN EPISTLE TEACHES: The church is the very *body of Christ*, and is therefore the *fullness of God*.

> . . . the church, which is his body, the fullness of him that filleth all in all (Ephesians 1:22, 23).

II. DISPENSATIONAL TEACHINGS: The church is not even mentioned in the Old Testament.

PAUL'S EPHESIAN EPISTLE TEACHES: The church was mentioned in the Old Testament as early as Genesis 2:24. For Paul quotes the passage from Genesis 2:24, and then says that this verse was spoken concerning Christ and the church.

> For this reason a man shall leave his father and mother and be joined to his wife, and the two shall become one." This is a great mystery, and I take it to mean *Christ and the church* (Ephesians 5:31, 32 RSV).

III. DISPENSATIONAL TEACHINGS: Israel and the church are separate bodies and are to remain so.

PAUL'S EPHESIAN EPISTLE TEACHES: God took two "men" (Israel's believing remnant and Christian Gentiles) and made the *two* of them into one "*man*." Now, therefore, there are no longer *two* bodies, but *one*.

> For he is our peace, who made both one, and brake down the middle wall of partition, having abolished in his flesh the enmity, even the law of commandments contained in ordinances; *that he might*

> *create in himself of the two one new man*, so making peace; and might reconcile them *both* in *one body* unto God through the cross, having slain the enmity thereby (Ephesians 2:14-16).

IV. DISPENSATIONAL TEACHINGS: National Israel will carry out God's main purpose during a future millennial period.

PAUL'S EPHESIAN EPISTLE TEACHES: The *church* is God's main instrument for carrying out his plans. This—the plan that the church would be the *fullness* of God (Eph. 1:23)—was according to the *eternal purpose* of God, and *has been realized* in Christ Jesus.

> To the intent that now unto the principalities and the powers in the heavenly places might be made known *through the church* the manifold wisdom of God, *according to the eternal purpose* which he purposed in Christ Jesus our Lord (Ephesians 3:10, 11).

Both Darby and Scofield taught that Israel was a *type* of the church. They went on to teach, however, that the church was not prophesied in the Old Testament, and that the type was never meant to have a fulfillment. This is indeed difficult to reconcile, a type without an antitype. In fact it is the only such type in their entire system. All other types, they say, were fulfilled through Christ.

To say, as dispensationalists do, that the church is parenthetic while national Israel is the eternal "chosen people" of God is to violate an important rule of hermeneutics. This is to make the type more important than its antitype. Someone has well said that a shadow can not cast a shadow. Israel was the shadow, the church is the substance. Abraham is the father of all the righteous; yet one must never lose sight of the fact that it is not through Abraham that one *becomes righteous*, but rather it is through Abraham's Seed "which is Christ" (Galatians 3:16).

So instead of the church being a temporary thing in the plan of God while national Israel is the main piece on the chessboard, actually the opposite is true. National Israel was chosen as a channel *for a limited time*. In other words, national Israel was the parenthesis which dispensationalists class the church as being. Many scriptures, in the Old Testament as well as in the New, plainly state that Israel's was a temporary role lasting only until the first coming of Christ. Indications that Messiah was to take over the scepter of Israel are given as early as the book of Genesis:

The sceptre shall not depart from Judah, Nor the ruler's staff from between his feet, *Until Shiloh come; and unto him shall the obedience of the peoples be* (Genesis 49:10).

The coming of Shiloh (Messiah) was longingly looked for by all the patriarchs and prophets of the Old Testament period. In John 8:56 our Lord reminded the unbelieving Jews that Abraham had prophesied the first advent: "Your father Abraham rejoiced to see my day; and he saw it, and was glad." To apply this verse to the second coming of Christ is to completely ignore the context in which it was spoken.

National Israel was characterized by three things—nationality, law, and circumcision. Again these were for a limited time only. These were shadows or types of our Lord's earthly ministry and the church. A statement by Phillip Mauro (*The Gospel of the Kingdom*, p. 81) sheds light on this fact.

> It is appropriate here to point out that one of the glaring errors of "dispensational teaching" is the failure to recognize what the New Testament plainly reveals, namely that names which God temporarily gave to the shadowy and typical things of the Old Covenant, belong properly and eternally to the corresponding realities of the New Covenant. Thus we are given the proper meaning of "Jew" (Rom. 2:28, 29); "Israel" (Rom. 9:6; Gal. 6:16); "Jerusalem" (Gal. 4:26); "Seed of Abraham" (Gal. 3:29); "Sion" (I Peter 2:6; Heb. 12:22; Rom. 9:33). Likewise it is made known that according to the New Covenant meaning, "the tribes of Jacob" are those who are Jews inwardly, that is to say, the entire household of faith (James 1:1; Acts 26:7).

Shiloh came nearly two thousand years ago, took over the scepter from national Israel, and began his reign in the hearts of his people. At that time the types faded in the pure light of the Substance to which they had pointed. Although the unbelieving part of Israel still held on to the shadows of nationality, law, and circumcision, the Israel of God (Galatians 6:16) condemned their continuance (Romans 6:14; 7:4; 10:4; Galatians 3:23-26; 4:9-11; 5:6). Having become the great Antitype of national Israel, the law, circumcision (Romans 2:28, 29; Philippians 3:3; Colossians 2:11), and the prophets, our Lord formed the believing part of Israel (Romans 11:5) into the Christian church. Nor was this an impulsive innovation; it was fulfillment of that which had been in the eternal plan of God (Compare Gen. 12:3, 22:18; Gal. 3:7-9, 14, 16, 27-29; Eph. 3:4-6).

Some are troubled by the fact that some of these Old Testament promises were *eternal*, yet ceased to be in effect. The Bible is its own interpreter. That is, we arrive at the meaning of any passage by a comparison of Scripture with Scripture. Looking at the Old Testament use of the word "eternal" one finds that it must be interpreted according to the radius of time being dealt with. An eternal priestly promise was in effect just as long as the priesthood existed; a legal eternal promise was in effect only so long as the law was in effect; an eternal promise to national Israel was in effect just as long as God dealt with Israel as a nation; an eternal promise with reference to the temple was binding upon God until the very second the temple ceased to exist; an eternal promise given under the old covenant was in effect during the entire life of the old covenant. Theological pandemonium has grown out of the attempt to make promises made under the law binding upon God long after the law has served its purpose in God's program.

Perhaps an illustration might help at this point. Let us say that a nation is on the gold standard and promises to stand behind its money forever. Then let us say that nation, by an act of congress, decides to change its money system. It is no longer on the gold standard, but is now using a completely different system of exchange. Gold may suddenly become worthless. Confederate money after the Civil War well illustrates this point.

The writer had the experience of serving with a tank battalion during World War II. During the Hitler regime the mark was the standard money in Germany. However, after the defeat of Hitler the money was completely changed by the Allies. Our soldiers went into many bombed-out banks after the Nazi surrendered. Many a soldier found bills which under Hitler's rule would have been worth thousands of marks. Now the soldier had a nice souvenir, but it was worthless. Why? Because new money had been printed. So with most eternal promises of the Old Testament. With the close of the Old Testament, God's program moved into an entirely different era.

Old Testament promises were eternal or everlasting for the duration of time God decreed to use a given method of dealing with his people. The duration usually was known to God alone. Israel's *national* promises were given during the period of the law and were eternal so long as the law was in effect. With the coming of Christ into the world, the period covered by the promises came to an end, and, therefore, the promises are no longer binding upon God. Paul speaks in II Corinthians 3:13-18 of the non-eternality of the law, and says in verse 14 that it is done away in Christ.

In II Chronicles 7:16 it is recorded that God promised to live in Solomon's house forever; yet that house was destroyed and does not exist today. Did God break his promise? No, "forever" meant for as long as the house stood.

The same is true with reference to the priesthood as instituted during the Old Testament era. In many passages—of which Exodus 40:15 and Numbers 25:13 are examples—we are told that the house of Aaron constituted an *everlasting* priesthood. All Protestant Christians are agreed that the old priesthood came to an end and was replaced by Jesus, who became our High Priest. The book of Hebrews makes this fact quite clear. So that the priesthood of law was everlasting *only as long as the law was in effect.*

In dealing with Genesis 13:15, which reads "For all the land which thou seest, to thee will I give it, and to thy seed *for ever*," Adam Clarke (*Clarke's Commentary*, Vol. I, p. 99) says:

> . . . and this was always the design of God, not that Abram himself should possess it, but that his posterity would, *till the manifestation of Christ in the flesh.* And this is chiefly what is to be understood by the words *for ever, ad olam*, to the end of the present dispensation, and the commencement of the new. *Olam* means either *eternity*, which implies the termination of celestial luminaries; or *a hidden, unknown, period, such as includes a completion or final termination, of a particular era, dispensation, etc.;* therefore, the first is its *proper* meaning, the latter its *accommodated* meaning (italics mine).

In dealing with Genesis 17:8, which reads: "And I will give unto thee, and to thy seed after thee, the land of thy sojournings, all the land of Canaan, for an *everlasting possession;* and I will be their God," Clarke has this comment:

> Here *olam* appears to be used in its *accommodated meaning*, and signifies the completion of the Divine counsel in reference to *a particular period or dispensation.* And it is literally true that the Israelites possessed the land of Canaan till the Mosaic dispensation was terminated in the complete introduction of that gospel . . . (Clarke's Commentary, Vol. I, p. 114).

There is a sense in which every eternal or everlasting promise never comes to an end. This is in fact the true sense in which these words are used throughout the Bible. If this proper sense were understood, many of our differences would immediately clear up. We refer to the fact that most if not all promises, covenants, ordinances, etc., of the Bible have different *forms* through which they pass. The all-wise God who gave them knew of these forms at the time he inspired his writers to use the words "eternal," "everlasting," "forever." While every *form* has its "end," *the actuality, of which the form is only one phase, never ends.*

Illustrations could be picked at random of everlasting things instituted by God which have passed through different forms, each form having its definite end. Among such illustrations might be listed: law, Sabbath, circumcision, kingdom, priesthood, the Israel of God. These by no means exhaust the list, but certainly they are among the more pronounced scriptural examples of the point being made. Each illustration listed—law, Sabbath, circumcision, kingdom, priesthood, God's chosen people—was definitely instituted and pronounced by God himself to be eternal. Each illustration listed has gone through *developments* (forms); and, while the realities themselves remain, in new form, the developments have long since ceased to exist.

The forms through which these everlasting things develop are essentially three in number: (1) from their inception until the first advent of Christ; (2) from that advent (*at which time each one developed into a much higher form*) until the second coming of Christ to earth; (3) from that second coming (which is yet future) they will be developed into the Eternal State which will have no end.

Viewing the entire Bible—while keeping in mind Paul's warning that the letter kills, while the spirit gives life—three definite points may be arrived at by way of concluding this chapter.

1.   God made a two fold covenant with Abraham, the main references to this covenant being recorded in Genesis 12:1-3; 15:1-21; 17:1-15; 22:1-19. This is called a two fold covenant because most of it involves believers from all nations, (compare Genesis 12:3, 22:18 with Galatians 3:7-9, 14, 16, 27-29). While a part of it was fulfilled in national Israel, the main parts of this covenant were spiritual and were ordained to include believers from every nation, including national Israel. Note that Israel was not even born at the time the Abrahamic covenant was first made.

2.   To implement his plans God arbitrarily chose Israel to be his peculiar people only until the first advent of Christ (Genesis 49:10). The Abrahamic covenant was renewed with Israel at

Sinai. This was not a separate covenant of works, but was the same covenant which had been given to Abraham, renewed with Isaac, Jacob, and now with Moses at Sinai. At Sinai Israel was also given conditional promises which applied to her alone and were to be in effect only until the coming of the church. By the time the church was established at Pentecost, all these national promises had been either literally fulfilled or invalidated through unbelief and disobedience. For a biblical account of these fulfillments see my book *The New-Covenant Israel* (Read Galatians 3:17, 19, 24).

3. Our Lord at his first advent (particularly through the death, burial, and resurrection) fulfilled the promises to national Israel and became their Deliverer (Luke 1:30-33, 76, 77; 2:25, 30). He was pointed to as the One through whom the Abrahamic covenant was to have its main fulfillment (Galatians 3:16).

He came as a Deliverer out of Zion (Romans 11:26) and all believing Jews (the remnant spoken of in Romans 11:5) were given power to become the sons of God. As many as received this opportunity, and indeed all who shall receive it during this present age, were formed into the Christian church which is the apex of all Jesus' suffering (Ephesians 1:20-23). Believers from every nation, including Israel, are being saved and brought into the church in fulfillment of Genesis 12:3; 22:18, and other such passages. This gathering will continue until our Lord returns to claim his vineyard which he has intrusted to disciples.

Envision for a moment the marshalling together of the church fathers, all the great Reformers, most of the outstanding contemporaries of J. N. Darby, and all the great theologians who labored to produce our Bible commentaries. If such a marshalling were possible, all these we have mentioned would line up with Paul and all the other apostles in condemning any teaching which makes the church a mere parenthesis. These men would say that the church for which our Lord bled and died was the very apex (as the body of Christ) of all God's planning. They would say, with Darby and Scofield, that national Israel was a type of the Christian church; then they would go on to the only logical conclusion, i.e., that all types have their antitype or fulfillment, and that the church, as the body of Christ, is the embodiment of all that national Israel typified.

IX

A SUMMARY

Dispensationalists begin by clearing the board of all opinions except their own; they dismiss as useless and false all historic interpretations. Next they divide the human race and the Bible into three distinct groups (this is convenient since any scripture which would otherwise refute their interpretation can be relegated to another "division" of Scripture). They add many arbitrary elements which are not supported by the Scriptures, such as extra captivities, extra kingdoms, extra covenants, extra judgments, extra ages, and so on and on. All of these stand or fall together. To disprove one of these premises is to collapse the entire theory.

Their cardinal teachings could be grouped into two main areas: the area of prophecy and the area of the church. Their major interest in prophetic teachings has to do with the prophecies concerning national Israel; most of these they hold to be yet future. With reference to the church, they make it a separate entity from national Israel and believe there are two separate plans for the two groups. Historic Christian theologians have held—as do the great majority of Christian thinkers today—that the nation of Israel was a type while the church is the antitype. That is to say that, rather than being two separate entities, one is a fulfillment or continuation of the other.

Darbyism (dispensationalism) is an unproved inference, which will not stand up under a close scrutiny of the Scriptures. Like many other movements within the history of Christianity this theory met with a widespread response because it struck out against apostasy. As one studies the history of this movement, one will find that there was a dearth of prophetic teaching when the Brethren movement originated about 1825 A.D. There also seems to have been a modernistic attempt to play down or deny completely the second coming of our Lord. This being the case, devout people grabbed quickly at a movement which filled this gap by emphasizing the second coming and a study of prophecy. This same situation explains the wide acceptance of the *Scofield Reference Bible*. Scofield, although not a Plymouth Brethren, was a devoted disciple of John Darby.

Like most movements, this one, which was dominated by Darby and later by Scofield, brought with it some unscriptural teachings. When there is a hunger on the part of the constituents for a certain type of legislation, it is all too easy for them to ignore undesirable "riders" attached to the bill, and, in their haste, to support more than they thought. This seems to have been the case with dispensational beliefs. Because of the great natural hunger on the part of many people for a return to prophetic teachings, many fascinating "riders" were attached by men such as Darby, and a "package deal" was subscribed to. Our attempt today is to "hold fast to that which is good" about the Darbyite teachings but to smooth off the rough unscriptural edges.

Most conservatives today would not subscribe *in toto* to all the teachings of Luther, Calvin, the Pietists, the Separatists, the Puritans, or any other such individual or group in history. Yet we feel that each of these groups has made contributions and has done much to awaken the church out of lethargy at given times in history.

Our point is that we ought to give the Plymouth Brethren credit where credit is due, but that we ought to be willing to admit they too "were men like ourselves." And we ought to be willing to hold their good points without being slaves to every jot and tittle of their doctrine. This will be hard for some to do, because many of these men, especially Scofield, have been almost literally canonized and it is considered by many to be sacrilegious to differ from them on a single point. Scofield's footnotes have been placed within the canon of the Bible itself and he carries the same weight in the minds of some as does the apostle Paul! Many Protestants have fallen into the practice of the Roman Catholic church by having extra-biblical "canonized saints" who speak *ex cathedra* and are beyond any court of appeal.

Many men, however, have gone into the dispensational movement only to leave it after further examination because of these extra-biblical teachings which were foisted upon every member of that school of thought. These men are still firm believers in predictive prophecy and look for the literal second coming of Christ. They have not left the Bible; they have simply left Darbyism and Scofieldism. George E. Ladd lists many such men in his book, *The Blessed Hope*.

We look, longingly, for the Blessed Hope of all believers, i.e., the literal, bodily return of our Lord in glory. At that coming we expect all graves to be opened. All the wicked from every generation, along with the wicked then living, will be judged and cast into eternal torment. Taking part in the judgment will be the saints from all ages; for all believers will have been signalled by the trump of God (I Thess. 4:16, 17) to be caught up to meet the Bridegroom in the air. His royal train will not stop in mid-air, but he will "bring his (raptured) saints with him" as he continues on to earth. Immediately after the cleansing judgment of all the earth, every believer, of every generation, will cast his crown at Christ's feet as all believers enter into the Eternal State with him.

"Even so come, *Lord* Jesus."

APPENDIX
*THE BIBLE WITHOUT COMMENT
—Proverbs 30:5,6

Most Protestants, certainly all evangelicals, accept the Scriptures as an all-sufficient guide in matters of practice and doctrine. It is at this point, in fact, that Protestants differ most from the Roman Catholic religion. Whereas Protestants accept only the Scriptures as authoritative, the Roman Catholic Church accepts the Scriptures plus tradition.

It is also axiomatic that Protestants have always refused to have any extra-canonical writings inserted in the Bible itself. They consider the canon as having closed the revealed Scriptures. John, in the Revelation (22:18, 19), was inspired to speak with authority and finality when he said dire consequences would attend any additions to or subtractions from the inspired text.

Although many Protestant groups gain much help from extra-biblical writings, such as the Didache, Apostles Creed, et cetera, these have never been permitted by evangelicals to be equated with sacred Scriptures; and they would never be permitted insertion within the Word of God. Roman Catholics have drawn much criticism from evangelicals because of their presumption in adding apocryphal writings to canonized Scriptures. The Jews have been thought equally presumptious in equating their Talmud with the Word of God.

One of the paramount contributions of the Protestant Reformation was the return to the Scriptures as the Christian's final earthly authority. The Reformers rebelled against all extra-biblical teachings as binding upon Christians. Many Protestants have even expressed regret that the name of King James was associated with the Protestant translation, even though this has never been looked on as a part of the Bible itself. The Protestant philosophy has always been—as stated by such outstanding translators as the British and Foreign Bible Society and the American Bible Society—"Without Note or Comment."

Knowing all the above to be true, the writer had a startling dream recently. He dreamed that Harry Emerson Fosdick had gathered up all of his own private notes which he had jotted down

*This article, written by the author for publication in *The Baptist Leader*, Nov., 1959, is presented here as it appeared in that magazine, even though a small part of the material is duplicated in the present book.

while studying the Bible, and had sent these notes to a publisher with instructions to incorporate them into a printing of the Holy Bible. Fosdick had carefully instructed the publisher as to where each of these private notes was to be inserted. Some of them were to appear as footnotes, some as marginal references, some as chapter headings, and in some cases Fosdick had even pried apart some verses of Scriptures in order to insert his own interpretation between them. And when this "Bible" came off the press, according to the dream, it did not carry the title *Holy Bible*, but was called the *Fosdick Reference Bible*.

Needless to say, the publication of the *Fosdick Reference Bible* caused a furor in nearly all Protestant circles. The Fundamentalist paper, *Knife of the Spirit*, carried an editorial under the following caption: "Liberal Minister Tampers With Word of God." The editor went on to point out how we were to be guardians of the faith once delivered to the saints, how that God would remove from the Book of Life the name of any person who added to or took from the inspired text. He further elucidated our great Protestant heritage, pointing up the fact that it was through bloodshed the Reformers won back our New Testament heritage, which had been transgressed by Catholic and Jew alike. He called upon all those who love the Lord to raise their voices in protest against this great apostasy.

An incredible dream? Indeed. Yet, how similar is the dream to the actual happening during the early part of the twentieth century. Many who cherish the Bible as the infallible Word of God go all out to perpetuate the teachings of the *Scofield Reference Bible*. Does the fact that Scofield was conservative in his theology change the picture when his name is substituted in the dream for that of Harry Emerson Fosdick? Was Scofield exempt from the scriptural warning in Revelation 22:18,19? Here is a man, whose ideas probably otherwise would be virtually unknown today, who has made himself a legend and guaranteed himself a hearing by inserting his private opinions within the Bible itself, thereby causing them to be read as a part of the Word of God. Many know the *Scofield Bible*, in fact, better than they know the Holy Bible!

Scofield's footnotes and his systematized schemes of hermeneutics have been memorized by many as religiously as have verses of the Bible. It is not at all uncommon to hear devout men recite these footnotes prefaced by the words, "The Bible says . . ." Many a pastor has lost all influence with members of his congregation and has been branded a liberal for no other reason than failure to concur in all the footnotes of Dr. Scofield. Even many ministers use the teachings of Scofield as tests of orthodoxy! Charles G. Trumbull, late editor of the *Sunday School Times*, spoke of the *Scofield Bible* in the following terms, in his book, *The Life Story of C. I. Scofield:* "God-planned, God-guided, God-energized work" (p. 114).

Albertus Pieters has this to say concerning the *Scofield Bible*, in his pamphlet entitled, *A Candid Examination of the Scofield Bible:*

> Through its influence there have arisen here and there "tabernacles" and "undenominational churches," composed of people no longer at home in the established orthodox denominations, because they do not get there the sort of teachings they find in the Scofield Bible. In many other churches, where this development has not yet reached the point of separation, the presence of Sunday-school teachers and others who consider themselves illuminated by the Scofield Bible beyond their pastors, form a troublesome element. Periodicals like the "Sunday School Times" and the "Moody Bible Institute Monthly" frequently refer to it, and always with an air of having spoken the final word, if they can quote a passage from it to support their views (pp. 4,5).

Who is this man who has had such a great influence upon the theological thinking of our generation? Biographical material concerning him is sparse indeed. From available material one can learn that Cyrus Ingerson Scofield (1843-1921) was educated in Tennessee, served valiantly under General Robert E. Lee, became a successful lawyer, was converted to the Christian faith in the year 1879, three years later—without any formal theological training—was ordained to the ministry by the Congregational denomination, and began to wield a mighty influence through his writings, which culminated in the publication of the *Scofield Reference Bible* in 1909.

The phenomenon of the wide influence of Scofield is heightened when one discovers that his teachings were taken almost *in toto* from John Nelson Darby. Darby was the outstanding leader among the Plymouth Brethren about 1830, and his "rediscovered truths" differed radically from the cardinal teachings of historic Christianity as held by the church fathers and Reformers.

(1)   Perhaps the major difference between Scofield and Darby on the one hand, and the historic Christian theologian on the

other, relates to their teaching concerning the Christian church. Historic Christian teaching is that national Israel was a type of the church and, since the first advent, has been superseded by the church. Scofield and Darby teach that, while Israel was indeed a type of the church, there has never been an antitype, or fulfillment, of the type (nor was there ever meant to be, according to Scofield). This is probably the only type in the Scofield system without a fulfillment! He teaches that the church is a parenthesis, i.e., something God is doing only while his work with national Israel has been postponed. When Jesus returns at the second coming, the church will be taken to heaven, and then God will return to the more important work with his "earthly people," Israel. God has two bodies (or peoples) a heavenly body (the church) and an earthly body (Israel) (S.R.B. p. 989).

(2) Another cardinal difference lies in the doctrine of the kingdom. Historically, the Christian teaching has been that there is one kingdom made up of all believers from both the Old Testament period and the New. This kingdom is a present reality, but will be consumated, or perfected, only upon the second coming of Jesus, Scofield teaches that there are two kingdoms; he distinguishes between "kingdom of heaven" and "kingdom of God" in spite of the fact that the two are used interchangeably throughout the New Testament. The kingdom which most Christians believe exists today has not yet begun, according to Scofield, and cannot begin until the second coming of our Lord to earth. Whereas most Christians believe the Bible teaches a present kingdom, which is spiritual in nature and includes both Jew and Gentile believers in Christ, Scofield finds it to be a future kingdom, which will be mainly political, material, and Jewish in nature (S.R.B., pp. 997, 1343).

(3) Following the general resurrection, say most Christians, there will be a final judgment (the sheep-goat judgment), at which time the believers will receive their rewards, and the unsaved will be cast into eternal punishment. Here again, Scofield begs to differ by saying there will be some five different judgments following the return of our Lord, and three of them are separated by a period of 1,000 years (coinciding with the millennium) from the remaining two. Actually, Scofield has seven judgments, but two of them take place in this life (S.R.B., p. 1351).

(4) At least one other major difference needs to be mentioned.

This has to do with the gospel, or God's good news. While the Christian church has always taught there is but one gospel, through which men are invited to God—and this included the Old Testament period as well as the New; Paul says that the gospel which he preached also had been the means of Abraham's salvation (see Gal. 3:8)—Scofield teaches that there are four gospels, each for a different age and purpose, and each having a distinct message (S.R.B., p. 1348).

The fact that these differences involve cardinal doctrines—the correct interpretation of which are necessary to an understanding of the Bible itself—makes it imperative that every student of the Scriptures re-examine the teachings of Scofield in the light of Paul's injunction, "What saith the scripture?" To do this is not to doubt the honesty or integrity of the late Dr. Scofield. Nor is it to deny that he was a conservative Bible student, who did much good for the cause of our Lord. It is merely to admit that C. I. Scofield was also a "man" like ourselves. Even the great apostle Peter made such a statement concerning himself. The following statement from *The Coming League and the Roman Dream*, by the late Harry Rimmer, himself an outstanding Bible teacher and evangelist, is ample proof of how even trained ministers can become enamored by the Scofield theories:

> For twenty years I also believed and taught that the Roman Empire would be restored in the last days of the age in which we live . . . I must confess that in so doing I depended largely upon the ideas and interpretation which I had imbibed from great and godly teachers, in whom I had unlimited confidence. I did not realize that I was teaching interpretation of the text in place of the Word itself, and had never made an exhaustive study of the Scriptures involved in this idea . . .

> I went over these prophecies again and was finally led to see that my only authority for maintaining that the Roman Empire would be rebuilt was a footnote in my favorite edition of a study Bible. So for twenty years I had taught as a prophecy of God's Word a human conclusion based upon an ambiguous paragraph (pp. 42, 43).

If we are to enjoy the benefits of our new interest in biblical theology, and if God is to have glory from this awakened interest in his Book, then the Book must be unfettered from all opinions of men, and the Holy Spirit must be given free reign to enlighten the hearts of those who study to show themselves approved unto God. We must again become a people of the Book, but that book must be "The Bible—Without Comment."

BIBLIOGRAPHY

Non-dispensational Books

ALLIS, O. T., *Prophecy and the Church*. Philadelphia: The Presbyterian and Reformed Publishing Co., 1945.

BARROWS, E. P., *Companion to the Bible*. New York: The American Tract Society, 1867.

BOETTNER, LORAINE, *The Millennium*. Philadelphia: Presbyterian and Reformed Publishing Co., 1958.

CAMPBELL, RODERICK, *Israel and the New Covenant*. Philadelphia: Presbyterian and Reformed Publishing Co., 1954.

CHAMBERLAIN, W. D., *The Church Faces the Isms*. (Edited by Arnold Black Rhodes.) New York: Abingdon Press, 1958.

COX, WILLIAM E., *The New-Covenant Israel*. Philadelphia: Presbyterian and Reformed Publishing Co., 1962.

HAMILTON, F. E., *The Basis of Millennial Faith*. Grand Rapids: Eerdmans, 1955.

HENDRIKSEN, WILLIAM, *More Than Conquerors*. Grand Rapids: Baker Book House, 1949.

HODGES, J. W., *Christ's Kingdom and Coming*. Grand Rapids: Eerdmans, 1957.

HUGHES, ARCHIBALD, *New Heaven and New Earth*. Philadelphia: Presbyterian and Reformed Publishing Co., 1957.

JOHNSTON, George, *The Doctrine of the Church in the New Testament*. New York: Cambridge University Press, 1943.

KIK, J. M., *Revelation XX* (1955) and *Matthew XXIV* (1948). Philadelphia: Presbyterian and Reformed Publishing Co.,

LADD, G. E., *Crucial Questions About the Kingdom of God*. Grand Rapids: Eerdmans, 1952.

LADD, G. E., *The Blessed Hope*. Grand Rapids: Eerdmans, 1956.

MORGAN, G. Campell, *Studies in the Prophecy of Jeremiah*. Chicago: Fleming H. Revell, 1931.

MAURO, Phillip, *The Gospel of the Kingdom*. London: Hamilton Brothers, 1928.

MAURO, Phillip, *The Seventy Weeks and the Great Tribulation*. Swengel, Pennsylvania: Bible Truth Depot, 1944.

PIETERS, Albertus, "A Candid Examination of the Scofield Bible." (pamphlet) Swengel, Penna.: Bible Truth Depot, n.d.

PIETERS, Albertus, *The Seed of Abraham*. Grand Rapids: Eerdmans, 1950.

QUISTORP, Heinrich, *Calvin's Doctrine of the Last Things*. Richmond: John Knox Press, 1955.

REESE, Alexander, *The Approaching Advent of Christ*. London: Marshall, Morgan and Scott, 1937.

ROBINSON, H. W., *The History of Israel*. London: Duckworth, 1938.

Non-dispensational Commentaries

Ante Nicene Fathers, Vol. I; Vol. V.

CARROLL, B. H., *An Interpretation of the English Bible* (Vol. XVII). Edited by J. B. Cranfill. New York: Fleming H. Revell, 1913.

CLARKE, Adam, *Clarke's Commentary*. New York: Abingdon-Cokesbury Press, n.d.

DAVIDSON, F., (Editor) *The New Bible Commentary*. Grand Rapids: Eerdmans, 1953.

Dispensational Books

BLACKSTONE, W. E., *Jesus is Coming*. Chicago: Moody Bible Institute, n.d.

BULLINGER, E. W., *The Foundation of Dispensational Truth*. London: Eyre & Spottiswodde, 1931.

CHAFER, L. S., *Dispensationalism*. Dallas: Dallas Seminary Press, 1951.

CHAFER, L. S., *The Kingdom in History and Prophecy*. Chicago: Fleming H. Revell, 1915.

CHAFER, L. S., *Systematic Theology*. Dallas: Dallas Seminary Press, 1948.

DARBY, John, *The Hopes of the Church of God*. London: G. Morrish, n.d.

EVANS, William, *Outline Studies of the Bible*. Chicago: Moody Press, 1913.

GORDON, S. D., *Quiet Talks About Jesus*. Chicago: Fleming H. Revell, 1906.

IRONSIDE, H. A., *The Mysteries of God*. New York: Loizeaux Brothers, 1908.

LARKIN, Clarence, *Rightly Dividing the Word*. Fox Chase, Philadelphia, Pennsylvania: C. Larkin, 1921.

NEATBY, W. B., *A History of the Plymouth Brethren*. London: Hodder and Stoughton, 1901.

NEWELL, W. R., *Romans Verse by Verse*. Chicago: Moody Press, 1938.

O'HAIR, J. C., *The Great Blunder of the Church*. Chicago: J. C. O'Hair, n.d.

PETTINGILL, W. L., *Bible Questions Answered*. Grand Rapids: Zondervan, n.d.

RYRIE, C. C., *The Basis of the Premillennial Faith*. New York: Loizeaux Brothers, 1953.

SCOFIELD, C. I., *What Do the Prophets Say?* Philadelphia: The Sunday School Times, 1916.

SCOFIELD, C. I., *The Scofield Reference Bible*. London: Oxford Press, 1917.

SMITH, O. J., *When the King Comes Back*. Wheaton: Sword of the Lord Publishers, n.d.

TURNER, W. G., *John Nelson Darby*. London: Hamond, 1944.

VEITCH, Thomas S., *The Story of the Brethren Movement*. London: Pickering & Inglis, n.d.